COGNITIVE OPERATIONS AND LEARNING DISABILITIES

COGNITIVE OPERATIONS AND LEARNING DISABILITIES

By

Dr. M.S. Gayathri Devi
M.Sc; M.Phil & Ph.D.
&
Dr. K.M. Mustafa
Director
Institute of Research in Learning Disabilities (IRLD)
Mahatma Gandhi University
(Kerala) (India)

DPH

DISCOVERY PUBLISHING HOUSE PVT. LTD.
INDIA

Published by:
Namit Wasan
DISCOVERY PUBLISHING HOUSE PVT. LTD.
4383/4B, Ansari Road, Darya Ganj
New Delhi-110 002 (India)
Phone : +91-11-23279245; 23253475; 43596065
E-mail : discoverybooksindia@gmail.com
discoverypublishinghouse@gmail.com
namitwasan9@gmail.com
web : www.discoverypublishinggroup.com

First Edition: **2020**

ISBN: 978-93-88854-27-6

Cognitive Operations and Learning Disabilities

Printed at:
Infinity Imaging Systems
Delhi

Preface

Millions of students struggle in school daily, because of serious learning problems. The causes are often unknown, specific problems can be difficult to pinpoint and the long-term effects hard to predict. The tension between demands or academic success and stubborn reality of a problem, make learning difficulties one of the most contentious topics in an increasingly competitive and educated society. A large number of educationists have been struggling for the recognition of fact that each child may have his/her own pace and learning requirements and forcing them. All into a single straitjacket is largely responsible for children dropping out of education altogether. This is always became a question in front of parents, teachers and researchers. A humble attempt was done by the authors in this direction and this book is the result of that attempt.

The book titled *"Cognitive Operations and Learning Disabilities"* has been written to be used as a research reference or as a referral text in Environmental and Neuro Psychological perspectives of LD.

The book is prepared based on the Research work carried out by Dr. M.S. Gayathri Devi under the supervision of Dr. K.M. Mustafa. The research problem of the study was Temperament, character and Executive functions among students with Learning Disability and without Ld. The study was a Neuro Psychological study, which is a unique one among the target group. Since the book is based on the research work, it clarifies a number of ideas closely related to temperament, character and executive functions of students with Learning Disabilities.

It is hoped that the book will be helpful and will serve as a useful resource for all stake holders. Since, this endeavour is a continues process, we would appreciate receiving feedback from the readers for further improvement.

Dr. M.S. Gyathri Devi

Dr. KM Mustafa

Acknowledgement

We express our deep gratitude to Dr. Mary K. Rothbart, Professor and the Author of Temperament theory, University of Oregon, she gave us the timely support, and advice to build the materials of our research work, advices and help throughout the research through mail. we also grateful to Prof. Samuel Putnam, Professor of the Psychology Department, Bowdoin University, for his timely response and comments and encouragement for the hard aspects of our research which intended us to widen our research from various perspectives. We would like to express our gratitude to Dr. M. Rosario Rueda, Associate Professor of Psychology, University of Granada, Spain, who gave us valuable supports and issuing available literatures to us to build the instrument of the research.

We are also thankful to all the Students and Head Masters/Head Mistresses of various schools in Kerala.

Above all we are thankful to the unseen power of almighty to finish this study properly, without the grace of Almighty it wouldn.t have been possible for us to develop this work within a short time limit.

Dr. MS Gyathri Devi

Dr. KM Mustafa

Abstract

Learning Disability is a neurological disorder that affects the brain ability to receive, process, store, and respond to information. It is seen from the literature review, the number of research conducted in the personality characteristics and executive functions of frontal lobe in the field of learning disabilities are very limited. Hence, the present study aimed to find out the temperament, character and executive functions among students with learning disabilities and without learning disabilities. The study has been carried out in two phases. In the first phase, the instrument, Early Adolescent Temperament Character Inventory (EATCI) was developed for assessing temperament and character of the participants. The expert team was validated the instrument and conducted pilot study to the instrument among 200 samples including students with learning disabilities. The item analyzed by the most common Cronbach alpha, which is ranged from 0.65 to 0.86. This attempt resulted in best output regarding the efficacy of EATCI. Hence EATCI applies for the present study. In the second phase, the EATCI and Wisconsin Card Sorting Test (WCST) were used to collect data. WCST is a well-established measure of executive function. WCST used for assessing higher-order cognitive functions that are related to the brain's frontal lobes such as multiple cognitive operations, which include strategic planning, organized searching, the application of external feedback to shift mental sets, and the inhibition of impulsive responses. The participants of the present study were 40 students with learning disabilities and 40 without learning disabilities. Descriptive research design was used for the present study. In order to find out the objectives and to test hypotheses, the statistical techniques such as; the comparison of mean, median, mode, skeweness, kurtosis and standard deviation, student 't' test and correlation were used for the present study. The findings of the study reveal that there is significant difference in temperament, character and executive functions among students with learning disabilities and without learning disabilities. The executive functions of students with learning disabilities had asignificant moderate relationship with temperament [especially in the dimensions of Effortful Control (EC), Surgency (S) and Affiliativeness (AF)] and character [Self- Directedness (SD) only]. In the case of students without learning disabilities, the executive functions had a significant moderate relationship with temperament only. The findings have been discussed in the light of available theoretical and empirical literature.

Keywords: Temperament, character, executive functions and learning disabilities.

Contents

1

Introduction

"Everybody is a genius. But if you judge a fish by its ability to climb a tree, it will live its whole life believing that it is stupid"

–Albert Einstein

There is no substantive proof that Einstein put forth this expression. However, this statement uncovers some enlighten thoughts to the general population. A fish is particular to swim eminently and its capacity to climb a tree is non-existent or simple. On the off chance that you judge on a man's unseemly norms, it will live them their entire life accepting is stupid. There are no one is born with no skills. Each one has their own potentials.The success is behind these potentials. Each individual child has the chance to succeed, paying little respect to regardless of whether they have incapacity.

In history, learning disabilities have been defined in numerous ways. The terms such as minimal brain dysfunction, word blindness, and dyslexia were initially used. Many adults that endured learning disabilities as a child turn out to be extremely fruitful later in life. With support and education, most will grow to be proactive, stable and determined adults with great future goals, steady jobs and caring families. Having learning disabilities does not spell vanquish for these adults. Challenges faced during childhood do not decide later achievement.

Children with learning disabilities lead to poor academic performance, which cause difficulties in later life in terms of job opportunities of the child. The presence of learning disabilities in a child with normal intelligence creates emotional problems for the child in terms of a sense of shame and guilt at not being able to perform well at studies. These in turn may lead to lowered self esteem and poor confidence in one's capabilities (Ginsburg, 1997; Kapur, 1995).

Everyone that had learning disabilitiesas a child will keep on having some impact of it for the duration of child's lives. However, through learning, practice and maturity, they be able to muddle through improved with issues and live the equivalent full, rich energy as any other adult. Many children with learning disabilities have trouble organizing, prioritizing and thinking flexibility. They have difficulty shifting also struggling to cope with unexpected changes in their routines, schedules, or homework and may be viewed or complained by their parents and teachers as stubborn, rigid or single minded. Students with Learning disabilities and Attention Deficit Hyperactivity Disorder (ADHD) often have difficulty to deal efficiently in self monitoring. They often forgot their goals and objectives. They may not select the best strategies for specific tasks, and they can't easily spot their errors. Instead, they might spend hours working, becoming increasingly frustrated because, they are not recognized when they are stuck and the need of shift to a different approach to complete the task, don't independently monitor or adjust their used strategies, don't know how to correct their errors properly and not aware of the approaches they are using to complete the tasks. For this sake, they need a strong supports from their family, friends, community, educational and career aspects. It also helps them to develop a healthy functioning of personality and brain.

The term personality may be very freely utilized by people in every day existence with one of a kind meaning. Some individuals refer to the physical appearance like height, weight, color, body built, dress, voice, and so on. Some other people consult with intellectual characteristics like intelligence, activeness, manner of speech, wondering and reasoning competencies, etc. It is also stated social traits like sociability, generosity, kindness, reservedness, and so on. On the basis of these traits they judge human beings as strong or weak personalities, top and bad personalities, and so forth. The link between personality (both biological and environmental dispositions) and learning problems are related to children's cognitive abilities. These abilities are control and regulate behaviours.

Temperament and character are the two dimensions of the personality. That is temperament is the influence of biological sides of the personality and character is the other side of the environmental influences. All individuals have individuality; each and every individual has an exclusive character. It is what makes us the person we are. Our personalities command our behaviour, thoughts, strong feelings and even our lifeless sentiments. It makes it likely to predict how an individual will act or react under distinct situations.

The concepts of temperament are necessary to understand the origins of personality development. Temperament describes the initial state from which personality develops and links individual differences in behaviour to underlying neural networks. Temperament and experience together "grow" a personality, which will include the child's developing cognitions about self, others, and the physical and social world, as well as his or her values, attitudes and coping strategies (Rothbart, 2007). Historically, temperament and personality have been studied as distinct sets of individual differences, with temperament consisting of more narrowly defined consistencies that appear earlier in life and with personality consisting of a broader range of consistencies that emerge later in life. Temperament and personality traits thus may be more elaborated forms of basic behavioural systems that appear across species. These temperament and personality traits may reflect individual differences in biological systems that have been selected through evolution and are shaped by individuals' life experiences (Nettle, 2006). Thus temperament is defined as individual differences in emotional, motor, and attentional reactivity measured by latency, intensity, and recovery of response, and self-regulation processes (Rothbart, 2007; Rothbart & Derryberry, 1981). To the extent that there is an overlap between the domains of temperament and cognition, evidence showing nutritional contributions to variability in cognitive performance may also apply to variability in temperament. Thus, evidence on the impact of varying intake of proteins and carbohydrates on performance of vigilance tasks (Christensen, 1996; Wachs, 2000).

According to Rothbart and colleagues, temperament may be divided into four factors called Effortful Control (EC), Surgency (S), Negative Affectivity (NA), and Affiliativeness (AF). Effortful Control (EC) comprises attention, inhibitory control and activation control. Surgency which loads positively on sensation seeking or high intensity pleasure, shyness and fear. Negative Affect (NA) stands for frustration, depressive mood and aggression. Affiliativeness (AF) is explains the positive emotionality or affiliation, pleasure sensitivity and perceptual sensitivity.

An individual's character continues to develop all through life, whereas much counts on inborn traits and early experiences. Character is furthermore reliant on a person's moral development. The character logic aspects of personality involve individual differences in self concepts about goals and values, in contrast to the temperaments that involve differences in automatic emotional reactions and habits. Such self concepts modify the significance or meaning of what is expected, thereby also changing emotional reactions. Accordingly, three character dimensions involve both an intellectual perspective about self/non self boundaries and an emotional perspective. According to Cloninger's psychological theory, character development involves changes in the propositional memory system, where as temperament involves individual differences in procedural memory (Cloninger *et al*, 1993).

The concept of character comprises the dimensions of self directedness, cooperativeness, and self transcendence. Self Directedness (SD) is associated with goal directedness, fluency of ideas, and sense of responsibility, self congruence, and self acceptance. Cooperativeness (CO) is associated with social acceptance, empathy, helpfulness, compassion for others, and conscience. Self-Transcendence (ST) refers to spirituality and fantasy (Drechsler *et al*, 2015).

The term executive function of frontal lobe refers to a set of cognitive abilities that are control and regulate behaviours. Executive functions are also regulates goal-directed behaviour. It includes the ability to initiate and stop activities, to monitor and change behaviour as required, and to plan future behavior when faced with novel tasks and situations. Executive functions permit us to approximates conclusions and adapt to altering positions. The proficiency to pattern notions and believe abstractly is often advised to the major components of executive function.

Executive functions are necessaryfor accurate adaptation and performance in real situations and also important for ones learning process. They allow individuals to initiate and complete tasks and to continuing in the face of challenges. Because the environmental situations can be changeable, executive functions are crucial to human ability to recognize the significance of unexpected situations and to make alternative plans rapidly when unusual events originate and hinder with normal routines. Therefore, executive function provides to success in work and school and allows people to manage the stresses of daily life. Executive functions additionally alter individuals to inhibit inappropriate behaviours. Individuals with poor executive functions usually have issues interacting with people since they'll say or do things that bizarre or attacking to others. Most people experience impulses to do or say things that could get them in trouble. When executive functions are impaired, however, these urges might not be suppressed. Executive functions are therefore important element of the ability to fit in socially.

According to study of Devi & Mustafa (2018) found that in certain areas of set shifting ability of frontal lobe executive functions among Students with Learning Disabilities compared to Students without Learning Disabilities have mild impairment. From their study clearly shows that the Students with Learning Disabilities are facing mild impairment in set shifting ability of frontal lobe executive functions than Students without Learning Disabilities. Shifting is involved in a wide range of abilities in the school (Clair-Thompson & Gathercole, 2006; Kraus, 2014). Children shift from one subject to another, from passage processing to questions, from reading to writing and from breaks to class time. When returning from school, they shift from the tasks to home setting. Apart from these shifting the working memory has more supports basic of executive functions in a wide range of school-home related and unrelated activities. Both the shifting and working memory can be affected by the speed of processing. Since the slower speed leads them the heavier the load on working memory and the slower the shifting process also becomes. Although, the study of Kraus (2014) examined these abilities in neuro psychological test on dyslexic students, which are different from real life functioning and it is appealing to think that the shifting ability itself might not be dysfunctional in participants with dyslexia and that its just affected their deficit in working memory, attention and in speed of processing also.

Among children with learning disabilities, temperament was more strongly related to teachability ratings than were student's cognitive abilities (Keogh, 1983; Teglasi, Cohn & Meshbesher, 2004). In academic instruction, importantly consider the characteristics of the child in relation to various tasks demands and conditions of learning and performances (Teglasi, Cohn & Meshbesher, 2004). Several studies have shown that temperament and character profile may differentiate various psycho-pathological issues showed abnormal profiles compared with normative sample. Both the children with autism spectrum disorders and children with ADHD showed with larger impairments in the autism spectrum group and in particular low scores for persistence and self-directedness in the ADHD group (Poustka *et al.*, 2011; Drechsler *et al.*, 2015). These findings are underline with earlier studies linked to the sensation seeking to conduct problems (Russo *et al.*, 1993). Hence the present study is intended to found the temperament, character and executive functions among Students with Learning Disabilities and Students without Learning Disabilities.

In the present study the temperament and character is assessed with the new instrument called Early Adolescent Temperament Character Inventory prepared by the investigator (EATCI) with the theoretical backup of Rothbart and Cloninger. In contrast, the model of temperament by Rothbart and collegues refers to executive control tendencies (Rothbart & Bates, 1998; Rothbart, Ellis, & Posner, 2004; Drechsler *et al.*, 2015) and which overlaps with Posner's neuropsychological concept of executive attention (Posner & Raichle, 1996). On the other hand, the executive function is assessed through Wisconsin Card Sorting Test (WCST) written by David A. Grant and Esta A. Berg. The WCST is often used to study executive functions, it is a neuropsychological test that engages the neural networks (Kimberg, D'Esposito & Farah, 1997; Lezak, 1983; Milner 1963; Kraus, 2014). The advantage of this test over other task that assess executive functions of a number of cognitive abilities, includes section, maintaining set, shifting tasks, rehearsal, attention and updating of task set information in working memory. Therefore WCST as considered a measure of executive functions (Corbetta & Shulman, 2002; Kraus, 2014). In a study shows that the Attention Deficit Hyperactivity Disorder (ADHD) group significantly shows a better performance than the Nonverbal Learning Disability (NLD) group on the majority of WCST variables with the exception of Failure to Maintain Set (FTMS) and Learning to Learn (LTL) scores. These findings recommend that while children with NLD indicates difficulty in abstract reasoning and perseverative in their way of approach to cognitive tasks, those with ADHD are quite adept at conceptual-level reasoning and display adequate cognitive flexibility. The results of this study support the notion that the behaviour of individuals with NLD is guided more by internal mechanisms, though the behaviour of individuals with ADHD seems to be more (Morais, 2000).

NEED AND SIGNIFICANCE OF THE STUDY

An individual with learning disabilities often have difficulty incomprehending the effects of his actions. They are more likely to act in certain way without thinking of its consequences. They have the tendency to act first and think about the action later. They are facing difficulty to adjust with the society and relationship with the peer groups. These are caused to some mistakes in their personality development. Children with learning disabilities have so many behavioural problems and they are having difficulty to cope with others and the educational systems.

Theories and methods from modern cognitive neuroscience have guided inquiry into the cognitive operations and neural mechanisms behind performance on the Wisconsin Card Sorting Test, one of the most extensively used tests in the history of clinical and experimental neuropsychology. It was originally developed to assess abstract reasoning ability and the ability to shift cognitive strategies in response to changing environmental contingencies (Berg, 1948, Grant & Berg, 1948). The acknowledgment of deficient brain functioning in children with learning disabilities has become more widely accepted particularlywith the advent of research evaluating the functioning of the brain. A discussion of the most recent findings about the neural structures involved in reading may highlight the various aspects of the learning process that need to be evaluated. Several studies revels that temperament has also been linked to different neurotransmitter systems. Character on the other hand is believed to be environmentally influenced, dependent on individual's experiences, influenced by cultural and social influences. Both the temperament and character share a common underlying neural base with the executive functioning tasks. The study of learning disabilities can be traced to several diverse disciplines including psychology, medicine, linguistics and education. Researchers and practioners in all of these specialized fields have made important contributions to the study of learning disabilities. Many studies are present in the field of learning disabilities but no one measure their neuropsychological issues, especially executive functions and their characteristics of personality. Here is the significance of this present study.

STATEMENT OF THE PROBLEM

Students with Learning Disabilities have neurological deficits. Thus it causes problems in their everyday functions and behaviour, especially in their developing personality and higher order functions. There are a lot of prior researches are trying to explore these problems of Students with Learning Disabilities.But there is no research results connected with the inherited dispositions (temperament), environmental influences of the dispositions (character), and higher order functions (executive functions) of children with learning disabilities. Temperament, character and executive functions were having neuropsychological bases. Thus this research study is an attempt to explore the temperament, character and executive functions of Studentswith and without Learning Disabilities. Hence the research problem stated as *"Cognitive Operations and Learning Disabilities"*.

SCOPE OF THE STUDY

The Students with Learning Disabilities have been suffering with intimate and personal care more widely especially,in educational systems. The government policies are not provide sufficient help and supports for them. They are ignored in school systems. It creates more complex issues to their existed causative factors, that is, the genetic and environmental factors. From this point the study leads to find out their neuropsychological deficits and its relationships to their personality. Since research works are very rare in this field, it is hoped that the result of this study would be highly beneficial in the field of government authorities, special educators, psychologists, clinical psychologists, parents, teachers, and public.

DELIMITATIONS OF THE STUDY

The study will confine itself with the availability of sample of Students with Learning Disabilities in Kollam, Pathanamthitta and Kottayam districts between the age group of 13 to 16 considered as early adolescence. The study initiated to find out the major aspects of temperament and character, and its measurements delimited to the Early Adolescent Temperament Character Inventory (EATCI) and Wisconsin Card Sorting Test (WCST).

OPERATIONAL DEFINITIONS

Temperament refers to the automatic emotional responses to experience and is moderately heritable (i.e. genetic, biological) and stable throughout life. The four measured Temperament dimensions are effortful control (EC), Surgency (S), Negative Affectivity (NA) and Affiliativeness (AF).

Character refers to self-concepts and individual differences in goals and values, which influence voluntary choices, intentions, and the meaning and salience of what is experienced in life. Differences in character are moderately influenced by socio-cultural learning and mature in progressive steps throughout life. Character takes into account the psychology of the development of personality. The three measured Character dimensions are Self-directedness (SD), Cooperativeness (CO), and Self-transcendence (ST).

Executive Function refers to the higher-order cognitive functions that are related to the brain's frontal lobes such as multiple cognitive operations, which include strategic planning, organized searching, the application of external feedback to shift mental sets, and the inhibition of impulsive responses.

Learning Disabilities refers to a neurological condition that interferes with a students' ability to store, process, or produce information. Learning disabilities can affect one's ability to read, write, speak, spell, compute math, reason and also affect a person's attention, memory, coordination, social skills and emotional maturity.

OBJECTIVES OF THE STUDY

1. To find out the dimensions of temperament among Students with Learning Disabilities.
2. To find out the temperament among Students with Learning Disabilities.
3. To find out the dimensions of character among Students with Learning Disabilities.
4. To find out the character among Students with Learning Disabilities.
5. To find out the dimensions of temperament among Students without Learning Disabilities.
6. To find out the temperament among Students without Learning Disabilities.
7. To find out the dimensions of character among Students withoutLearning Disabilities.
8. To find out the character among Students without Learning Disabilities.
9. To find outcertain selected executive functions among Students with Learning Disabilities.
10. To find outcertain selected executive functions among Students without Learning Disabilities.
11. To find out the relation between dimensions of temperament and certain selected executive functions among Students with Learning Disabilities.
12. To find out the relation between temperament and certain selected executive functions among Students with Learning Disabilities.
13. To find out the relation between dimensions of character and certain selected executive functions among Students with Learning Disabilities.
14. To find out the relation between character and certain selected executive functions among Students with Learning Disabilities.
15. To find out the relation between dimensions of temperament and certain selected executive functions among Students without Learning Disabilities.
16. To find out the relation between temperament and certain selected executive functions among Students without Learning Disabilities.
17. To find out the relation between dimensions of character and certain selected executive functions among Students without Learning Disabilities.
18. To find out the relation between character and certain selected executive functions among Students without Learning Disabilities.

19. To compare the dimensions of temperament among Students with Learning Disabilities and without Learning Disabilities.
20. To compare the temperament among Students with Learning Disabilities and without Learning Disabilities.
21. To compare the dimensions of character among Students with Learning Disabilities and without Learning Disabilities.
22. To compare the character among Students with Learning Disabilities and without Learning Disabilities.
23. To compare certain selected executive functions among Students with Learning Disabilities and without Learning Disabilities.
24. To compare the dimensions of temperament with respect to age.
25. To compare the temperament with respect to age.
26. To compare the dimensions of character with respect to age.
27. To compare the characterwith respect to age.
28. To compare certain selected executive functions with respect to age.
29. To compare the relationship of temperament and executive functions among Students with Learning Disabilities and without Learning Disabilities.
30. To compare the relationship of character and executive functions among Students with Learning Disabilities and without Learning Disabilities.

HYPOTHESES OF THE STUDY

All hypotheses are set in null form (H0).

1. There will be no relation between the dimensionsof temperament and certain selected executive functions among Students with Learning Disabilities.
2. There will be no relation between the total temperament scores and certainselected executive functions among Students with Learning Disabilities.
3. There will be no relation between dimensions of character and certain selected executive functions among Students with Learning Disabilities.
4. There will be no relation between the total character scores and certain selected executive functions among Students with Learning Disabilities.
5. There will be no relation between dimensions of temperament and certain selected executive functions among Students without Learning Disabilities.
6. There will be no relation between the total temperament scores and certain selected executive functions among Students without Learning Disabilities.
7. There will be no relation between dimensions of character and certain selected executive functions among Students without Learning Disabilities.

8. There will be no relation between the total character scores and certain selected executive functions among Students without Learning Disabilities.
9. There will be no significant difference indimensions of temperament between Students with Learning Disabilities and without Learning Disabilities.
10. There will be no significant difference in the total temperament scores between Students with Learning Disabilities and without Learning Disabilities.
11. There will be no significant difference indimensions of character between Students with Learning Disabilities and without Learning Disabilities.
12. There will be no significant difference in the total character scores between Students with Learning Disabilities and without Learning Disabilities.
13. There will be no significant difference in certain selected executive functions between Students with Learning Disabilities and without Learning Disabilities.
14. There will be no significant difference in dimensions of temperament with respect to age.
15. There will be no significant difference in the total temperament scores with respect to age.
16. There will be no significant difference in dimensions of character with respect to age.
17. There will be no significant difference in the total character scores with respect to age.
18. There will be no significant difference in certain selected executive functions with respect to age.
19. There will be no relation between the correlation coefficient of total temperament scores and certain selected executive functions among Students with Learning Disabilities than that of Students without Learning Disabilities.
20. There will be no relation between the correlation coefficient of total character scores and certain selected executive functions among Students with Learning Disabilities than that of Students without Learning Disabilities.

METHODS IN BRIEF

A research design is the arrangement of condition for collection and analysis of data in a manner that aims to combine relevance to the research purpose with the economy in procedure. Since the study is an attempt to find out the temperament, character and executive functions. The descriptive research design has been used for the present study. The study evolved two phases. In the first phase, the expert team validated the instrument and then conducted pilot study to the instrument statistically verified and comprised of data collection, analysis, interpretation and report preparation. The second phase, prepared final form for this use.

Population

Students with and without Learning Disabilities attending in various schools in Kerala are the population for the present study. Samples selected from the different schools of Kollam, Pathanamthitta, and Kottayam districts of Kerala of the age group 13 to 16.

The Sample

The random sampling method is used for the present study.In the first phase, among 200 samples including Students with Learning Disabilities and Students without Learning Disabilities were used for the pilot study where as in the second phase, the sample consisted of total 40 Students with Learning Disabilities and 40 without Learning Disabilities they are studying under class 10.The subjects were of the age group 13 years to 16. The samples were selected after the screening by using IQ test and learning disabilities screening tests. The sample was included as sample in the study if he/she has average or above average Intelligence Quotient (IQ), for Students with Learning Disabilities, if they have the certificate oflearning disabilities from government authorized clinical psychologist and those who attempted learning disabilities screening test and IQ test from the investigator. The Students with Learning Disabilities were excluded from sample for the convenience of the study, that are,if the students who suffer from visual, hearing, intellectual challenges or other social, emotional, family problems, if he/she is under medication, those who have no certificate from the government officials, he/she was denied screening test and IQ test and he/she returned incomplete or improperly answered questionnaire.

Instruments

1. Personal data sheet(prepared by the investigator).
2. The Early Adolescent Temperament Character Inventory (EATCI) (prepared by the investigator).
3. Wisconsin Card Sorting Test (WCST) (The WCST was written by David A. Grant and Esta A. Berg. The Professional Manual for the WCST was written by Robert K. Heaton, Gordon J. Chelune, Jack L. Talley, Gary G. Kay, and Glenn Curtiss).

The Statistical Techniques

The statistical techniques applied for the present study are;

1. Descriptive statistics such as; mean, median, mode and standard deviation, skewness, kurtosis, minimum and maximum scores.

2. To test of group mean difference of variables were calculated by student's t-test.
3. The product moment of correlation coefficient has been used to measure the relationship between the variables.

LIMITATIONS OF THE STUDY

The study has certain limitations, that has to be taken into account.

1. The sample selectedonly from thethree districts of Kerala.
2. The study assessed only in the areas of strategic planning, organized searching, utilizing environmental feedback to shift cognitive sets, directing behavior toward achieving goal and modulating impulsive responding of executive functions.

OUTLINE OF THE RESEARCH REPORT

The research reports are organized in five chapters. In the first chapter is introduction of the research report which discussed the objectives, hypotheses, operation definitions, method adopted, need, significance and scope of the study. In chapter 2 comprised details the depth of the related literature to discover what is already known about the research area. This chapter unfold in the major heads; an overview of learning disabilities, incidence and prevalence of learning disabilities,genetics of learning disabilities, neuropsychology of learning disabilities, personality, concept of temperament and character, executive functions of frontal lobe, and temperament, character and executive functions. Chapter 3 gives detailed account of general methods adopted to discuss the objectives. Chapter 4 gives the major results and discussions of the study. The final 5th chapter gives a brief summary of the entire work.

2

Review of Literature

"A successful book is not made of what is in it, but what is left out of it"

–Mark Twain

INTRODUCTION

A review of literature is related evaluative information already found in the selected study, which describe, and classified the selected study. It will help to determine the nature of the research. It synthesises the information in that literature into a summary. Review of literature is what is more vital to focus on distinction in opinions, contradictory findings or proof and also the different interpretations given for their deductions and dissimilarities by different authors. In some situations, an investigation of these components can help one realize may facets of a complex topic and other times, such analysis can lead to a new possibility that can be studied upon in the present research.

This chapter provides a summary of previous investigations into temperament, character and how it can be associated or influenced to the executive functions of the students with and without learning disabilities. In this chapter, first look at the brief explanation of the concept and different theories of learning disabilities, and how it associated with personality and executive functions.

Learning Disability: An Overview

The term learning disabilities refer to a neurobiological issue in at least one or more of the essential procedure engaged with understanding spoken or written language. This brain variance may influence an individual's ability to speak, listen, read, write, spell, reason, organize information, or do mathematical calculations.

Many people prefer to mix up or confused to use of the term "learning disorder", "learning difficulty or problems", and "slow learner" instead of "learning disabilities". In UK, the two terms of learning disabilities and learning difficulty are used interchangeably in the field of health and social care. Some Australian states used the term "learning difficulties" for all students who struggling in literacy and numeracy. But learning disabilities should not be confused with the term "learning difficulty or problem". This term is primarily the result of visual, hearing or motor handicaps of intellectual disability, emotional disturbances or environmental cultural or economic disadvantages (ldamerica.org). On the other hand slow learner is children who have below average intelligence, whose thinking skills have developed significantly more slowly than the norm of his/her age. They will go through the same developmental stages as similar to other children, but will do so at a significantly slower rate. However this development while being slower nevertheless is relatively even (dsf.net.ac). The investigator currently used the term students with learning disabilities because; learning disabilities generally speaking are of average or above average intelligence.They have difficulties in specific areas of academic achievement as a result of impairment in one or more of the cognitive processes related to learning. There often appears to be a gap between the children's potential and actual achievement. That is why learning disabilities are referred to as 'hidden disabilities' because the individual looks perfectly 'normal' and seems to be a very bright and intelligent person, yet they may be unable to demonstrate the skill level expected from a similar age group.

Learning disabilities is discovered over all the ages, races, ethnic background and in all socio-economic classes, but it's manifested differently in different people. In 1960's numerous young kids were having with learning problem reported in western schools. This started appeal grave vigilance towards the children's having learning disabilities. An increasing number of children were discovered incapable to cope with schoolwork particularly with reading, writing and arithmetic. These young kids were otherwise brilliant, fairly articulate in their verbal expression and did not appear to have any form of mental retardation, sensory impairments or visual impairment. Samuel Kirk he first used the term learning disability to describe these children. Many scientific studies and research was conducted in the field of learning disabilities. In the past decade has witnessed a significant improvement in the quality of research on learning disabilities. Much of this recent research has been longitudinal in nature, thus opening the door to the identification of better predictors of different types of Learning Disabilities, their prevalence, their developmental course, and their response to intervention.

Definition of Learning Disability

Formulating definition of learning disabilities that is usual to the entire has been difficult. Some influential definitions are given below.

Minimal Brain Dysfunction

The first formal definition proposed at a national level was the minimal brain dysfunction (MBD) definition. Diagnosticians did not like the task of detecting minimal brain dysfunction. Moreover, special educators found that labels connoting a medical aetiology were not useful in planning educational interventions.

According to Clements (1966), "these aberrations may arise from genetic variations, biochemical irregularities, perinatal brain insults or other illness or injuries sustained during the years which are critical for the development and maturation of the central nervous system, or from unknown causes" (Mercer & Pullen, 2009).

National Advisory Committee on Handicapped Children Definition

The National Advisory Committee on Handicapped Children (NACHC) was formed in 1968 to develop an acceptable definition. Under Kirk's leadership, the committee submitted a definition that was incorporated into Public Law 91-230, the specific learning disability act of 1969.

"Children with special learning disabilities exhibit a disorder in one or more of the basic psychological process involved in understanding or in using spoken or written languages. These may be manifested in disorders of listening, thinking, talking, reading, writing, spelling or arithmetic. They include conditions, which have been referred to as perceptual handicaps, brain injury, minimal brain dysfunction, dyslexia, developmental aphasia, etc. They do not include learning problems, which are due primarily to visual, hearing, or motor handicaps, to mental retardation, emotional disturbance or to environmental disadvantage" (U.S.Office of education, 1968).

Individuals with Disabilities Education Act Definition

The regulations of U.S.Office of Education in 1977 have seen only minor revisions in the definition of a specific learning disability. The Individuals with Disabilities Education Act (IDEA) regulations in the 2006 code of federal regulations, which are based on the 2004 reauthorization of IDEA, state: "Specific learning disability means a disorder in one or more of the basic psychological processes involved in understanding or in using language, spoken or written, that may manifest itself in the imperfect ability to listen, think, speak, read, write, spell, or to do mathematical calculations, including conditions such as perceptual disabilities, brain injury, minimal brain dysfunction, dyslexia, and developmental aphasia ... specific learning disability does not include learning problems that are primarily the result of visual, hearing, or motor disabilities, of mental retardation, of emotional disturbance, or of environmental, cultural, or economic disadvantage".

This definition is currently used for administering programs for individuals with learning disabilities.

National Joint Committee on Learning Disabilities Definition

In 1981, the National Joint Committee on Learning Disabilities (NJCLD) representatives with exception of the [Association for Children and Adults with Learning Disabilities (ACLD)] reached agreement on the following definition:

"Learning disabilities is a generic term that refers to a heterogeneous group of disorders manifested by significant difficulties in the acquisition and use of listening, speaking, reading, writing, reasoning or mathematical abilities. These disorders are intrinsic to the individual and presumed to be due to central nervous system dysfunction. Even though a learning disability may occur concomitantly with other handicapping conditions (e.g., sensory impairment, mental retardation, social and emotional disturbance) or environmental influences (eg., cultural differences, insufficient/inappropriate instruction, psychogenic factors), it is not the direct result of those conditions or influences" (Hammill, Leigh, McNutt, & Larsen,1981).

In 1988, the NJCLD slightly modified its earlier definition. The revised definition indicates that the disorders "may occur across the life span" and states that " problems in self-regulatory behaviours, social perception, and social interaction may exist with learning disabilities but do not by themselves constitute a learning disability" (National Joint Committee on Learning Disabilities, 1988).

Association for Children with Learning Disabilities Definition

The leaders of the Association for Children with Learning Disabilities (1986) rejected the NJCLD definition and wrote their own definition:

"Specific learning disabilitiesis a chronic condition of presumed neurological origin that selectively interferes with the development, integration, and/or demonstration of verbal and/or nonverbal abilities. Specific learning disability exists as a distinct handicapping condition and varies in its manifestations and in degree of severity. Throughout life, the condition can affect self esteem, education, vocation, socialisation, and/or daily living activities.

Brief History of Learning Disability

Learning disabilities is a young field and its history is largely one of the past very few years. Essentially all of the relevant history of learning disabilities took place within the twentieth century. To understand learning disabilities, it is helpful to examine the development of the field of learning disabilities from historical perspective.The major events of historical aspects of learning disabilities occurred within four periods: the foundation period (1800-1960), the emergent period (1961-1974), the solidification period (1975-1986) and the turbulent period 1987- present).

Beginning in the early 1800s, investigate in Europe started on the relationship of the brain and mental impairment. Most early researchersduring this period concentrated on brain pathology. Scientists such as Franz Joseph Gall, Carl Wernicke, John Baptiste Bouillaud, Henry Head, and James Hinshelwood contributed to the understanding of learning difficulties during the foundation period.

Later in the foundation period, the focus of research moved from grown-ups to children, and scientists started translating theory to educational practice. Samuel T. Orton, an expert in neurology, guessed that one side of the braincommanded the language process (Orton, 1937).He suspected that children with language disabilities who had no self evident brain damage had neglected to establishhemispheric dominance.

Although little empirical evidence supports Orton's speculations concerning brain dominance, instructors keep on using his remediation methodologies since they are powerful with some children with written language problems.Among the researchers who developed and publicized these strategies are Marion Monroe, Anna Gillingham, Bessie Stillman, Samuel a. Kirk, Grace Fernald, and Romalda Spalding. Collectively, these researchers gave rise to multisensory teaching (Mercer & Pullen, 2009). By the 1950s, public attitudes toward education had progressed to the point that most Americans concurred that education should to be for all children. These states of mind gave the stimulus to a legal foundation for giving such an education.

The emergent period was a pivotal time for the field of learning disabilities. The term Minimal Brain Dysfunction (MBD), presented in the 1960s, advanced the idea of minor brain injury or dysfunction and connected it with learning issues. The term incorporated minimal physical injury and included new ideas, for example, brain structure variations, biochemical anomalies, and slow maturation patterns (Smith, 1994). The National Advisory Committee on Handicapped Children (NACHC) was formedin 1968 to build up a definition. Under Samuel A. Kirk leadership, the committee built up a definition that was utilized as a part of Public Law 91-230, the Specific LearningDisabilities Act of 1969.

At 1963, a national conference had been wanted to make national association. At this 1963, conference in Chicago, Kirk presented the term learning disabilities. Parents, who had been disappointed with the current terms, acknowledged the new term energetically and framed the Association for Children with Learning Disabilities (ACLD, now the learning inabilities relationship of America, LDA).

The acknowledgment of the term learning disabilities and the development of intervention programs came immediately contrasted and the speed of events before the 1960s. During this period, several intervention programs were made with the assumption that a learning disability was the after effect of either psychological processing or visual-perceptual processing deficits (Hallahan and Mercer, 2001).

Wonderful development in the field of learning disabilities on all fronts portrays this solidification period, and specifically, the section of Public Law 94-142 was a significant highlight. The emphasis on the definition of the term during the 1975-1977 periods was extreme and questionable. After hearings, the regulations for Public Law 94-142 were published in 1977 (U.S. Office of Education, 1977), significantly impacting the learning disabilities field. The enactment perceived learning disabilitiesas a crippling condition, qualified for every one of the services and rights accessible to other special education categories.

In 1986, Public Law 99-457 was passed, expanding the rights and provisions of Public Law 94-142 to newborn children and preschoolers and requiring the improvement of an Individualized Family Service Plan (IFSP) for these children. Likewise Madeleine Will (1986) advanced the Regular Education Initiative (REI), which expressed that students with learning disabilities (and other exceptionalities) should be taught in the general classroom and kept up that pullout programs were ineffectual. Numerous learning disabilities specialists couldn't help contradicting this position and still do today.

The field of learning disabilities advanced during the foundation period, the emergent period and the solidification period. For sure, the field was immovably settled with parents associations, professional associations, and research centres. In spite of the fact that the field was more develop, numerous inquiries stayed unanswered.

Many special educators (Hammill, 1993; Kauffman, 1994; Mather and Roberts, 1994; Moats and Lyon, 1993) trust the field of learning disabilities entered a turbulent transition or reform period in the late 1980s. Kauffman keeps up that special education by and large, and learning disabilities particularly, are stuck in an unfortunate situation since special educators have neglected to convey steady and quality services. The development to incorporate learning disabilities under the umbrella of mild disabilities threatens the existence of the field (Mather and Roberts, 1994).

In spite of the fact that not especially new, the term Nonverbal Learning Disabilities (NLD) is as of now accepting consideration (Telzrow and Bonar, 2002). A NLD is a neurologically based disorder and regularly shows serious social issues (Lerner, 2003).

Social, political, economic, and professional powers of progress are bringing about significant impacts on the field of learning disabilities. Luckily, the field of learning disabilities has a gigantic pool of capable experts, individuals with learning disabilities, and parents of children with learning disabilities who acknowledge difficulties and work overwhelmingly to discover better responses to complex issues.

Historical Figures in the Field

- L. Bender: Developed one of the early tests of visual motor performance - the Bender Visual Motor Gestalt Test.

- W. Cruikshank: Built on the theories of Strauss and Werner to develop a teaching method for use with brain-injured children-the reduced stimuli environment.
- M. Frostig: Studied visual motor performance and developed an assessment to measure such performance in several areas.
- J. Gallagher: Described the uneven pattern of cognitive development exhibited by certain children as a "developmental imbalance" and suggested that this imbalance may be once cause for learning disabilities.
- K. Goldstein: Identified a relationship between brain injury in soldiers and certain types of learning problems including such perceptual problems as reversals and figure-ground confusion.
- N. Kepheart: Influenced the visual motor theories by development of a test of visual motor performance - the Purdue Perceptual Motor Survey.
- Kirk: Coined the term learning disability and developed an assessment instrument to aid the identification of learning disabilities in children.
- Orton: Studied delayed language among children and hypothesized that a lag in hemispheric specialization in the brain may cause learning disabilities.
- Strauss: Working with Heinz Werner identified the similarity between the types of perceptual problems experienced by the brain- injured soldiers studied by Goldstien and perceptual problems in slow-reading children. Identified this group of children as slow in reading because of brain injury rather than retardation.
- Werner: Worked with Alfred Strauss

Varied Characteristics

Students with learning disabilities show several types of learning and behavioural traits, and no individual exhibits all of the traits. Some have disabilities in mathematics, whereas others excel in mathematics. Attention disorders are symptomatic problems for many students with learning disabilities but not for all. Further, certain kinds or characteristics are more likely to be exhibited at certain age levels. Young children are more likely to be hyperactive than adolescents. In addition, deficits are manifested in different ways at different age levels. For example, an underlying language disorder may appear as delayed speech problem in the pre-schooler, as a reading disorder in the elementary pupil, and as a writing disorder in the secondary student.

These characteristics are also found among children with other disorders and disabilities. The implications of each of these learning and behavioural characteristics is complex.

- Disorders of Attention: Does not focus when a lesson is presented; short attention span, easily distracted, poor concentration; may display hyperactivity.

- Poor Motor Abilities: Difficulty with gross motor abilities and fine motor coordination (Exhibits general awkwardness and clumsiness).
- Psychological Processing Deficits: Problems in processing auditory or visual information (Difficulty interpreting visual or auditory stimuli).
- Lack of Phonological Awareness: Poor at recognizing sounds of language cannot identify phoneme sounds in spoken language).
- Poor Cognitive Strategies for Learning: Does not know how to go about the task of learning and studying; lacks organization skills; passive learning style (do not direct their own learning).
- Oral Language Difficulties: Underlying language disorders (problems in language development, listening, speaking, and vocabulary).
- Reading Difficulties: About 80% of students with learning disabilities have disabilities in reading (problems in learning to decode words, basic word-recognition skills, or reading comprehension).
- Writing Difficulties: Poor in tasks requiring written expression, spelling, and handwriting.
- Mathematics: Difficulty with quantitative thinking, arithmetic, time space, and calculation facts.
- Social skills: Does not know how to act and talk in social situations; difficulty with establishing satisfying social relationships and friendships.

Types of Learning Disabilities

Now a days, various terms are used to describe specific learning disabilities. A person may exhibit one or more of them. Some of them are as follows (codes provided are ICD-10 and DSM-5TM, respectively).

According to Diagnostic and Statistical Manual for Mental Disorders-5TM (F81.0-F81.2/315.00-315.1)

315.0 F81.0) with impairment in reading:

- Word reading accuracy
- Reading rate or fluency
- Reading comprehension

Note: *Dyslexia* is an alternative term used to refer to a pattern of learning difficulties characterized by problems with accurate or fluent word recognition, poor decoding, and poor spelling abilities. If dyslexia is used to specify this particular pattern of difficulties, it is important also to specify any additional difficulties that are present, such as difficulties with reading comprehension or math reasoning.

315.2 (F81.1) Withimpairment in written expression:

- Spelling accuracy
- Grammar and punctuation accuracy
- Clarity or organization of written expression

315.1 (F81.2) with impairment in mathematics:

- Number sense
- Memorization of arithmetic facts
- Accurate or fluent calculation
- Accurate math reasoning

Note: *Dyscalculia* is an alternative term used to refer to a pattern of difficulties characterized by problems processing numerical information, learning arithmetic facts, and performing accurate or fluent calculations. If dyscalculia is used to specify this particular pattern of mathematic difficulties, it is important also to specify any additional difficulties that are present, such as difficulties with math reasoning or word reasoning accuracy.

According to the International Classification of Diseases-10 (ICD-10), the learning disabilities is included in the criteria of F80-F89 Disorders of psychological development. Which is named in ICD-10 are specific developmental disorders of scholastic skills that are given below:

F81 Specific developmental disorders of scholastic skills
F81.0 Specific reading disorder
F81.1 Specific spelling disorder
F81.2 Specific disorder of arithmetical skills
F81.3 Mixed disorder of scholastic skills
F81.8 Other developmental disorders of scholastic skills
F81.9 Developmental disorder of scholastic skills, unspecified

INCIDENCE AND PREVALENCE OF LEARNING DISABILITIES

It is hard to know the genuine prevalence rate of particular learning disabilities. Nonetheless, the learning disabilities classification presently represents 52% of all students with disabilities served in a special education under the Individuals with Disabilities Education Act (IDEA). Between 1976-77 and 1996-97, the number of students serving as learning disabilities increased from 797,213 to 2,259,000, a 283% increase (Macmillan, *et al.*, 1996).

Important considerations regarding the determination of LD prevalence were presented by MacMillan (1993) and Lyon (1996). In a discussion of operationalsing disability definitions MacMillan described prevalence rate as referring to the total percentage of the population that is affected by a disorder while detection rate refers to the number of known or identified cases. For learning disabilities, prevalence and detection rates may, indeed likely do, differ. Depending on the stringency of identification criteria, prevalence estimates for learning disabilities have varied from as low as 1% to as high as 30% of the school-age population (Lerner, 1993). Mercer (1991) suggested that those with severe specific learning disabilities might comprise approximately 1.5% of students, while the inclusion of students with mild learning disabilities could raise that figure to about 4 or 5%. Other studies focusing on a specific classification of learning disabilities identify 5-8% of school age children with arithmetical disabilities (Geary, 2003) and 5-17.5% with dyslexia (Shaywitz, 1998). It is still estimated that 52% of all students being served in special education have a classification of LD with an actual count exceeding 2.5 million (Kavale & Forness, 2003).

Around 6 percent of students may display particular learning disabilities and will require special education interventions. Prevalence rates of students with specific learning disabilities including math and written expression are hard to evaluate given the current lack of research prove (Cook L, *et al.*, 2001).

Mogasale *et al.*, (2012) conducted a cross-sectional multi-arranged stratified randomized cluster sampling study to measure the prevalence of specific learning disabilities, for example, dyslexia, dysgraphia and dyscalculia among elementary school kids in a South Indian city among childrens aged 8-11 years from third and fourth standard. And found that the prevalence of particular learning handicaps was 15.17% in sample children, while 12.5%, 11.2% and 10.5% had dysgraphia, dyslexia and dyscalculia individually. This investigation proposes that the prevalence of SpLDs is at the higher side of past estimations in India.

A cross-sectional study to recognize learning disabilities in children with poor school performance and to break down their clinical profile over a period of 1-year from July 2013 to June 2014 conducted at Kannur Medical College, Anjarakandy and country zones of Kannur area in Kerala state, India, an aggregate 300 students with poor school performance were chosen by their class teachers. Out of the 300 students with poor school performances, parental view of learning issues was seen in 106 students. Post evaluation 39(13%) students had learning incapacity. Affiliation was found between low birth weight, preterm birth, dialect, social and engine formative deferral. Affiliation was additionally found between learning incapacity and consideration shortfall hyperactivity issue (Kumari & Barkiya, 2016).

GENETICS OF LEARNING DISABILITIES

Learning disabilities have traditionally been examined as neurological deficits intrinsic to genetic and other biological factors within the individual and not of environmental origin.

The earliest widely cited family pedigree study of reading disorder, conducted by Hallgren in 1950 (Pennington, 1991), consisted of a statistical analysis of dyslexia in 112 families. Among first-degree relatives (parents and siblings of an identified child), the risk for co-occurrence of this disorder was 41%, which is much higher than the usual prevalence estimates for the general population of 5-10%. Huston (1992), reporting on Hallgren's study, indicated that of the 112 families, in 90 families, one parent was dyslexic; in 3 families both parents were dyslexic; and in 19 families neither parent had

Friston, Liddle & Frack, 1991), orthography (Flowers, Wood & Nailer, 1991), phonology and semantics (Pugh, Constable, Shaywitz, Skudlarski, Fulbright, Katz, Shankweiler, Bronen, Gore & Fletcher, 1996).

However, a great deal of variability has been found then and between studies such that multiple sites within similar regions of the brain have been implicated in these processes (Poeppel,1996). However, current research is documenting the intimate connection between environment and neuroanatomical development (Dawson & Fischer, 1994; Hutenlocher, 1991). The pervasive effects of early environmental programming on the formation and pruning of neural networks and the theoretical relationship of this process to the occurrence of neurologically based specific learning disabilities are an area that is only beginning to be considered. Clinical studies have documented cases in which major structural deficits, even loss of an entire brain hemisphere, result in few observable signs of learning disability while many individuals with severe learning disabilities have no obvious structural deficits (Bigler, 1992; Satz, 1990).

Various studies have try to distinguish the neurological basis of learning disabilities, as far asright versus left hemisphere dysfunction. Adult strokes were begin to influences cognitive abilities such as scholastic aptitude, reasoning, memory clusters, written language, perceptual speed, (Aram & Ekelman, 1988), reading, language or verbal learning (Aram, Gillespie & Yamashita, 1990; Eden *et al.*, 1993; Leavell & Lewandowski, 1990), and arithmetic processing (Aram *et al*, 1990). Which is predicted that, as a result of immunological factors or genetic or epigenetic hormonal, the cortical language areas are disturbed in their development through migration disorders and unusual asymmetry, like that normal left hemisphere dominance does not develop, resulting in dyslexia in some children (Njiokiktjien, 1994). At the later stages of learning to read the proficient reader appear to depend on efficient left hemispheric verbal perceptual processes. Other evidence is offered that reaching in the early stages is dependent on right hemispheric dominance. Also that not all children employ identical strategies in learning to read, since some children adopt left hemispheric approaches and others right hemispheric strategies. The later are more alert to the perceptual properties of stimuli, exploring the visual features more systematically, resulting in slower but more accurate reading.

The left hemisphere strategies are faster readers, guess more readily and also examine the perceptual elements of the visual configuration more carefully. The association of chronic social difficulties linked with deficits in producing and understanding the emotional expressions, in paired with left-hemisphere signs, has been stated as the right hemisphere deficit syndrome (Voeller, 1995). Lower reading performance has also been incorporated with the right hemisphere (Aram & Ekelman, 1988; Aram *et al.*, 1990; Branch,

Cohen & Hynd, 1995; Cossu, Da Prati & Marshall, 1995; Ogden, 1996), as have visuospatial deficits (Tranel *et al.*, 1987) and mathematical problems (Branch *et al.*, 1995; Rourke & Conway, 1997; Shalev, Manor, Amir, Gross-Tsur & Wertman-Elad, 1995).

One of the first researchers into reading disability was Hinshel Wood (1917) who described three types of word blindness in adults which were due to damage in certain areas of the brain. One of these types was very common and formed the basis of his theory concerning congenital word blindness in children.

Later Hermann and Norrie (1958) also equated children with a reading disability with brain damaged adults with Gerstmann's syndrome where right-left confusion problems with finger localization and writing problems are evident. Their ideas were further extended by Kinsbourne and Warrington (1966) who considered that there were two types of children with specific reading disability- the Gerstmann group and the language group.

A problem with auditory-visual integration was first described by Birch and Belmont (1965) and forms the basis of a neurological theory put forward by them and Geschwind (1964). As integrative and associative functions of an auditory-visual nature are normally localized in the inferior parietal region, a congenital defect in this area could account for reading disability.

Another theory put forward by Witelson (1977). She maintains that dyslexic children have a different kind of hemispherical dominance or laterality pattern due to neural deficits. The theory attempts to account for the differing incidence of reading disability in boys when compared with girls, there being something like four to every one girl with reading problem. Specifically she maintains that dyslexic boys have cerebral hemispheres which both function as if they are right hemispheres, so they are good at form and colour perception but poor at language.

Writing is a complex activity requiring the coordination of several skills. Firstly, the writer has a body of material which he or she wishes to write about. Secondly, he or she has some ability to translate this information into meaningful language. Thirdly, there is appropriate execution of this meaningful language in handwriting. This last aspect, handwriting, is a highly developed skills which the young child executes slowly and with intense concentration.

Several researchers (Bryant and Bradley, 1980, 1983; Frith, 1980; Read, 1981) have expressed the view that writing is a language skill which is very different from reading. It is not the inverse of reading and probably both have different sources and development.

A further aspect of writing is its execution in handwriting. From the first stumbling copying of child's name to the flowing style of the adult, there is a gradual development of automaticity. The writing requires less conscious effort and becomes a precise skill. Luria (1973) has described the development of this skill as a functional development of various part of brain. He refers to the kinetic melody of handwriting as the functional integration of hand, the sensory and motor parts of the brain controlling movement, the eye and visual cortex, the language areas and the association areas, and the frontal cortex (the thinking part).

From a psychological point of view, it is absorbing interest to trace any link between cerebral insult and deficiency in number operations. Grewel's (1969) scholarly review of the acalculias (impaired ability to perform simple calculations) is recommended, and should convey some notion of the difference in views expressed over the last half century. His survey of the clinical evidence for the localization of lesion in the occipital, temporal, frontal and parietal lobes and disturbances in calculations, mainly in adults, is still a classic study.

German neurologist Gerstmann (1924) described a complex of four systems in which right-left disorientation, finger agnosia and deficiencies in writing and counting resulted from left parietal lesions.

Injuries in the right hemisphere, including the thalamic, medial and posterios cortical areas, affect spatial perception and visuo-spatial memory, which in turn impairs calculation skills (Ojemann, 1974).

Luria (1966) noted that adults with damage to the parietal-occipital areas of the brain demonstrated disturbances of spatial imagery, resulting in loss of ability to perform arithmetical calculations.

Hecaen (1972), on the other hand, found that right hemisphere lesions led to spatial dyscalculia, while bilateral disturbances led to acalculia. Critchly (1983) reported that left parietal lobe symptoms often gave rise to arithematical computation weaknesses, such as those found in individuals with Gerstmann syndrome. It should be pointed out that the use of these prefixes is used rather imprecisely by workers and that some caution should be exercised in translating the findings of number disorders in adults to that of children with development number retardation.

Dyscalculia has been extensively studied by neuropsychologist (Levin,1979), but the focus of interest has been on the nature of the disorder, rather than on its treatment. An analysis of errors made of acalculic individuals revealed that failure to use spatial representations, set out digits in their correct sequences, and copy out subtraction operations, were caused by parietal lesions.

Some specific areas of dysfunction have been identified in association with developmental dyslexia, namely, frontal lobe dysfunction (Heilman *et al.*, 1996), pointing immaturity in the myelination inside the focal sensory system (Condor, Anderson, and Sailing, 1995), left temporal dysfunctons (Cohen, Town, and Buff, 1988), and cerebellar hindrance (Fawcett, Nicholson, and Dean, 1996). The attentional issues related with a few cases of learning disabilities seem to have a generally dispersed neurobiological basis extending from the brainstem reticular activating system to the basal ganglia and on into the frontal cortex (Bakker, 1992).

A few subtypes of reading disabilities have been accounted for (Doehring, 1978; Doehring & Hoshko, 1977; Doehring, Trites, Patel, & Fiedorowicz, 1981; Fiedorowicz, 1986; Fiedorowicz & Trites, 1991; Trites & Fiedorowicz, 1976). Research has demonstrated that the locus of an anomaly in the brainis important,these abnormalities in different areas of the brain arerelated to different reading problems. Hence, the reason that one individual has difficulty reading may not be the same reason as another individual.

Individuals with nonverbal learning disabilities typically have well-developed auditory perception (including phonological awareness) and simple motor skills.They have primary neuropsychological deficits involving tactual perception, visual perception and complex psychomotor abilities and psycho-social functioning, also difficulties in processing novel information (Rourke & Fuerst, 1992, 1995, 1996; Tranel *et al.*, 1987). This kind of strengths and deficits has now been identified in individuals with a wide variety of congenital and developmental disorders and is associated with diffuse brain impairment, leading some investigators to speculate that it is characteristic of white matter disease or dysfunction (Rourke, 1995).

Kirk (1963) was generally coined the term learning disabilities. But that time several case studies presented and the results depicting that learning problems of a specific nature. Kussmaul (1877) was among the first scientists to report a patient who, although having number of visual impairment, was unable to read words.

Morgan (1896) reported that after 7 years of instruction, a 14 year old boy could read only, letters and single syllables. The adolescent's writing to dictation also was poor. In 1898 Bastian described another case with similar symptoms. Despite adequate speech and language skills, athletic prowess, and good arithmetic skills, this 18 year old boy consistently manifested word reversals in reading and severe deficiencies in spelling.

Fisher (1905), Hinshelwood (1909) & Stephenson (1905) reported at the turn of the century further emphasized the heterogeneous nature of specific learning deficits, with several of these case reports postulating the presence of a familial component that was contributing to the learning difficulties. Jackson (1906) described two additional cases and noted a greater frequency of specific reading problems among males than females.

Early Case Studies

In early 1900s Hooper *et al.* (1989) suggested that learning disabilities: (a) were present in children, adolescents, and adults with relatively intact cognitive functions, (b) occurred more frequently among males than females,

(c) were heterogeneous in terms of symptom manifestation, differently affecting reading, spelling and higher order cognitive functioning, (d) were generally unresponsive to traditional learning opportunities and instructional settings, (e) appeared to have a familial component, and (f) required a comprehensive clinical assessment for accurate diagnosis.

Single Factor Theories

Although most of these early case studies suggested that learning problems were heterogeneous in nature, nearly all of the research that followed primarily focused on single factor theories. Orton (1928, 1937), sought out to identify a single deficient process that contributed to the learning problem. Many works have been devoted to single factor theories. The three important theories are (1) delayed cerebral dominance, (2) visual-perceptual deficits and (3) auditory perceptual deficits and associated language inefficiencies.

1. **Delayed Cerebral Dominance:** Orton (1928, 1937), using an objective approach to assessment, described children who exhibited difficulties with letter sequences, letter differentiation, and letter juxtapositions. He attributed these difficulties to a neurodevelopment failure in establishing cerebral dominance. Based on his clinical observation that there was a higher incidence of reading problems in children with mixed handedness, Orton proposed that the left cerebral hemisphere failed to achieve functional superiority in these children. In turn, Orton stated that this was directly related to deficiencies in information processing, ultimately leading to problems in reading.

   Although not without merit, Orton's theory was oversimplified and illogically founded (Corballis & Beale, 1983) and his concept of incomplete (or delayed) cerebral dominance now has been refuted empirically (Benton, 1975; Kinsbourne & Hiscock, 1981). Instead, more complex theories of learning problems have emerged from hemispheric studies using dichotic-listening and visual-half-field paradigms (McKeever & Van Reventer, 1975).

2. **Visual-Perceptual Deficits:** closely related to Orton's delayed cerebral dominance model were several theories implicating deficits in visual-perceptual abilities (Bender, 1956, 1957; Frosting, 1964; Hermann, 1959; Kephart, 1971). Bender (1956, 1957) implicated poor figure-ground visual perception in reading deficits whereas Kephart (1971) and Frosting (1964) proposed that faulty visual-motor integration was the underlying cause.

   Data from Florida Longitudinal Project (Satz *et al.*, 1978) suggested that deficits in visual-perceptual and visual-motor functioning, particularly during kindergarten and early primary grades, were the best predictors of later learning problems. Vellutino (1979) noted that many visual-perceptual problems in both younger and older poor readers were secondary to deficiencies in verbal-medication strategies. Pirozzolo's (1979) work with eye movement patterns, the visual perceptual deficit model was unable to account for the multiple deficits found in many learning disabilities individuals.

3. **Auditory-Perceptual/Language Deficits:** Curtiss and Tallal (1988) have suggested that reading disabled children had poorer auditory perception, and that this adversely affected the development of phonic skills, efficient auditory processing and ultimately, reading performance.

   Vellutino (1979) and associates (Vellutino, Steger, Desetto & Phillips, 1975) presented evidence during verbal abstraction, and generalization of verbal information. Blank and Bridger (1966) obtained similar findings in their work with disabled readers and verbal classification more than 46 years ago.

   This theory continues to be prominent in the field of learning disabilities; however, other investigators have challenged these results (Hammil & Larsen,1974, Richardson *et al.*, 1977).

   The concept of learning disabilities has a long history, but it has been over only the past three decades that this concept has been a steady proliferation of research investigating its associated neuropsychological factors (Hooper & Willis, 1989: Rourkr, 1985). It is clear that neuropsychology plays a prominent role in contemporary thinking about learning disabilities (Gaddes, 1985: Hooper & Willis, 1989: Hynd, Connor & Nieves, 1988: Knights & Baker, 1976).

PERSONALITY

The term personality may be very freely utilized by people in every day existence with one of a kind meaning. Some individuals refer to the physical appearance like height, weight, colour, body built, dress, voice, and so on. Some other people consult with intellectual characteristics like intelligence, activeness, manner of speech, wondering and reasoning competencies, etc. It is also stated social traits like sociability, generosity, kindness, reservedness, and so on. On the basis of these traits they judge human beings as strong or weak personalities, top and bad personalities, and so forth.

The term "personality" comes from the Greek word 'persona' means mask. Masks were not used to conceal the identity of a man in the old Greek speaking theatres, rather, the covers were utilized to speak to or embody the character. One approach to comprehend personality is to take a look at how it has been characterized. In psychology, personality is viewed as an accumulation of emotional, cognitive and behavioural patterns special to a man that is relatively consistentover time.

A few psychologists have given their life to watching the scope of human body types and the related human personality attributes or disposition composes. These sacred typologies comprised of thoughts that physical make-up is hereditarily decided (Kretschmer, 1977) and were misusedduring the late 1930s in creating eugenic dispositions.

According to Eysenck, personality refers to the sum-total of the actual or potential behaviour-patterns of the organism, as determined by heredity and environment; it originates and develops through the functional interaction of the four main sectors into which these behaviour-patterns are organised: the cognitive sector (intelligence), the conative sector-3(character), the affective sector (temperament), and the somatic sector (constitution) (Eysenck, 1999).

Theoretical Overview of Personality

Hippocrates (460 B.C - 370 B.C.)

The idea of personality has been contemplated for not less than 2,000 years, starting with Hippocrates in 370 BCE, one of the ancient Greek theorists of personality. Hecreateda theory in light of the four components (air, water fire and earth) in which he accepted characteristics and their representation in four humors: blood, phlegm, yellow bile and black bile. "These fluids decide determine the nature of his body and because of them man is healthy or sick" (Strelau, 1998).

Galen (129-200 AC)

Later Centuries, the Greek physician and philosopher Galen based on Hippocrates' theory, recommending that the two diseases and personality contrasts could be clarified by imbalances in the humours and that every individual shows one of the four temperaments. Galen's theory was common for more than 1,000 years and kept on being mainstream through the middle Ages.

He explained the sanguine type (abundant supply of blood) as cheerful and optimistic, cheerful to be with and comfortable with his or her work. The cholerictype (yellow bile) is characterised by quick to act, hot temper, and regularly an aggressive nature. The phlegmatic type (phlegm) is represented by its slow, laziness, and calm. The melancholic type (emerging from dark bile) is characterised by individuals who have a tendency to be sad, even depressed, and take a skeptical perspective of the world (Strelau, 1998).

GordenAllport (1897- 1967)

According to Allport (1937) personality refers to the dynamic organisation within the individual of those psychophysicalsystems that determine his unique adjustment to his environment.

Atrait or disposition (a term synonymously utilized by Allport) represents 'biophysical facts' or 'psychophysical dispositions' is characterized as theoretical constructs that depicts a fundamental personality dimension that is moderately stableacross circumstances and time (Allport & Odbert, 1936, Cloninger S., 2000).

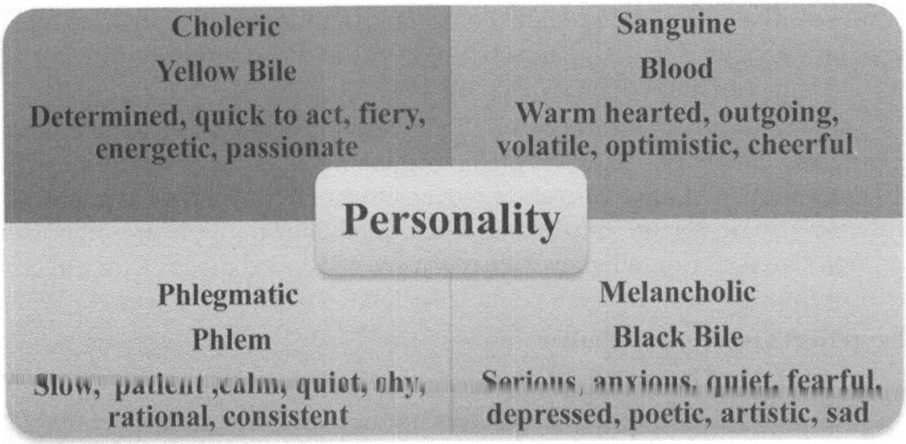

Fig. 2.1: Galen's description of personality types

Consistency of behaviour was a main theme by Allport and he recognized individual traits from common traits and (a) 'cardinal traits' that are spread over, dominating and shaping everything an individual does. Such traits are rarely seen because most individuals lack a single theme, to the point that shapes their lives. (b) 'Central traits' that unavoidably influence manybehaviours; and represent to a general characteristics found to some degree in everybody; and (c) 'secondary traits' which cause consistent behaviours yet don't influence behaviour across over time or situations to the degree of 'central traits. He argued that the self represents to a major focus of personalitygrowth; and expected personality as reason for behaviour being a component of heredity interacting with the environment [personality =f(Heredity) x (Environment)] (Brändström, 2009).

Hans J. Eysenck (1916-1997)

Eysenck utilized an indistinguishable terms from Jung-extraversion-introversion yet gave them an alternate meaning. Jung, who had first presented the idea, used introversion to represent the personality of schizophrenics and hysterics as models of extraversion (Eysenck, 1999).

Eysenck proposed a three-factor model of personality: extraversion (E), neuroticism (N) and psychoticism (P). Eysenck asserted that different variables found in the Big Five or the Alternative Five, for instance Agreeableness, Aggression, Activity and Sensation Seeking, are either blends of his E, N, and P or parts of them (Zuckerman *et al.*, 1993).

The three super-factors are characterized as far as observed intercorrelations between traits (Strelau, 1998). In this way extraversion, rather than introversion, is made out of such traits as sociability, liveliness, activity, assertiveness, and sensation seeking (Brändström, 2009).

Neuroticism, for which emotionality is utilized as an equivalent word, has the accompanying components: anxiety, depression, guilt feelings, low self-esteem, and tension. The contrary pole of neuroticism is characterized as defined as emotional stability (Brändström, 2009).

Psychoticism, the inverse of impulse control, comprises of such primary traits as aggression, coldness, egocentrism, impersonality and impulsiveness (Strelau, 1998). Likewise it can be depicted as a tendency towards nonconformity and social deviance, which implies a man who scores high in psychoticism does not need to be psychotic rather s/he will simply impart some common characteristics to them (Cloninger S., 2000).

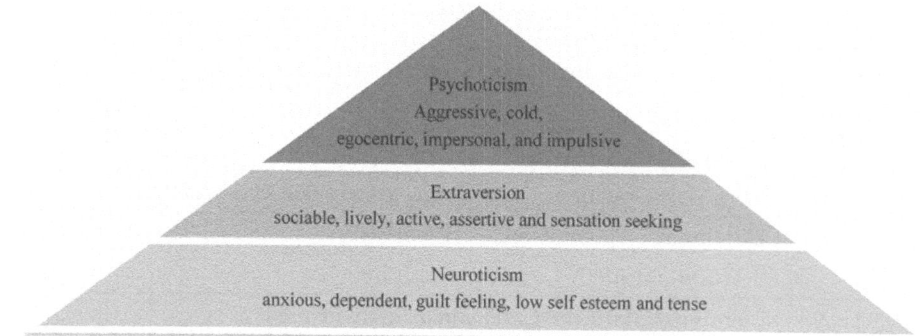

Fig. 2.2: Structure of Eysenck's three superfactors (Brändström, 2009)

Raymond Cattell (1905-1998) belived that true factors of personality should be found across different types of data, such as self-reports (S-data) and laboratory tests (T-data). Although they donot always produce identical numbers of personality factors, the different data sources do yield enough consistency to lend credibility to Cattell's system, which consists of 16 personality factors. In contrasts to Eyesenck, who developed one of the smallest taxonomies of personality, as judged by the number of factors, Cattell's taxonomy of 16 is among the largest in terms of the number of factors identified as basic traits. Much of research has been conducted on the personality profiles of persons in various occupational groups, such as police officers, research scientists, social workers and janitors (Larsen & Buss, 2005).

Cattell's legitimacy is a methodical description of personality traits in view of his assumption that" all aspects of human personality which are or have been of importance, interest, or utility have already become recorded in the substance of language" (Cattell, 1943). He built up his list of traits as far as adjectives from an assortment of sources accepting that so as to apply factor analysis to personality it is important to test widest possible range of variables; in this way establishing the 'factor analytic trait theories' of personality (Cloninger, 2000).

The pioneering work of Allport and Odbert's lexical approach started in the 1930s. The five factor model was emerged based on the combination of lexical and statistical approach. The five factor model has received the most attention and support from personality researchers, it is labelled the five-factor model, the big five and even in the humorous vein the High Five (Costa & McCrae, 1995; Goldberg,1981; McCrae & John, 1992; Saucier & Goldberg, 1996). The broad traits composing the big five have been provisionally named, surgency or extraversion, agreeableness, conscientiousness, emotional stability and openness-intellect (Larsen & Buss, 2005).

Table 2.1: Cattell's 16 personality factors

	16 Personality Factors
1.	**Abstractedness:** Imaginative versus practical
2.	**Reasoning:** Abstract versus concrete
3.	**Apprehension:** Worried versus confident
4.	**Rule-Consciousness:** Conforming versus non-conforming
5.	**Dominance:** Forceful versus submissive
6.	**Self-Reliance:** Self-sufficient versus dependent
7.	**Emotional Stability:** Calm versus high-strung
8.	**Sensitivity:** Tender-hearted versus tough-minded.
9.	**Liveliness:** Spontaneous versus restrained
10.	**Social Boldness:** Uninhibited versus shy
11.	**Openness to Change:** Flexible versus attached to the familiar
12.	**Tension:** Impatient versus relaxed
13.	**Perfectionism:** Controlled versus undisciplined
14.	**Vigilance:** Suspicious versus trusting
15.	**Privateness:** Discreet versus open
16.	**Warmth:** Outgoing versus reserved

Marvin Zuckerman, for one, battled that the distinction between temperament and personality regarding the context is neither clear nor significant and that the elementary characteristics or dimensions given to explain personality/temperament needs to go beyond describing ones vernacular to the behavioural significance of that trait. Zuckerman's personality traits are mainly focused on the term sensation seeking. These personality traits originated from temperament with sensation seeking for as "the seeking of varied, novel, complex and intense sensations and the willingness to take physical, social, legal and financial risks for the sake of such experience" (Zuckerman, 1994). He argued that sensation seeking is an ordinary trait of personality; and that "temperament is the genetically based foundations of personality, in light of a child's acquired predispositions for characteristic patternsof behaviour, including emotionality, activity and sociability" (Cloninger S., 2000). He created Sensation-seeking as a trait, characterizing it as an" optimistic tendency to approach novel stimuli and explore the earth" (Zuckerman, 1994).

Zuckerman's psychobiological theory of personality follows ahierarchical structure, top-to-bottom, that are; (1) traits, which are associated to (2)social behaviour, which are associated to (3) conditioning or observational learning, which are related to (4) physiology, then (5) biochemistry, then (6) neurology and lastly (7) genetics. Each level is a distinct component which needs to be studied on its own, however for an inclusive understanding of any level one cannot ignore the next level down which forms its foundation (Zuckerman, 1992; Zuckerman *et al.*,1993).

C. Robert Cloninger (1944 -)

In the 1980s Cloninger began to work together with Swedish researchers including M. Bohman and S. Sigvardsson. The research concentrated on collaborations between genes and environment and their effect upon personality attributes as key develops of psychopathological phenomena in selectedsamples and overall population samples (Cloninger *et al.*, 1981, 1982, 1984; Bohman *et al.*, 1981, 1982, 1984; Sigvardsson *et al.*, 1982, 1984). From these outcomes Cloninger went back to his own before work and wrote his first outline of a biosocial theory of personality (1986).

Cloninger needed to build up a general model of personality which could be connected to normal personality and in addition abnormal personality (Cloninger *et al.*, 1994). Cloninger describes personality as the "dynamic organization within an individual of the psychobiological systems that modulate adaptation to a changing environment" (Cloninger and Svrakic, 1997). The psychobiological systems are involved the systems that control cognition, emotion and mood, impulse control and social relations (Cloninger & Svrakic, 1997).

Cloninger's four factor modelsis a modern interpretation of the Galen's ancient four temperaments of bodily humours discussed previously: Melancholic (Harm Avoidance), choleric (Novelty Seeking), sanguine (Reward Dependence, and phlegmatic (Persistence) (Cloninger *et al.*, 1994). Cloninger's measurements of personality were proposed to give a differential analysis within the personality disorder populations and it appeared to offer a good description of conventional subtypes of personality disorders.

Cloninger built up a psychometric scale known as the Temperament Personality Questionnaire (TPQ), a self-report questionnaire, to test the above putative measurements and decide whether it could be a solid and stable model of personality. From studies about that contrasted the TPQ with other personality tests, different features of personality which were not represented in the temperament measurements were found to be lacking (Gillespie *et al.*, 2003). Therefore Cloninger's model was modified to incorporate the character components of personality: Self-directed behaviour, Cooperativeness and Self-transcendence. These were intended to assess individual difference in conceptual learning. In this manner the TPQ ended up known as the Temperament and Character Inventory (TCI), a 240-item measure that depends on his psychobiological theory of personality (Cloninger *et al.*, 1994). Cloninger currently had a seven-factor modal for both normal and abnormal personality.

Mary K. Rothbart (1940-)

Rothbart's study of individual differences in temperament has lasts for past four decades. The study also associated with the big five factor model. Her theory was concentrated on the temperament aspects of personality. Inspirations of her theory were her children's differences in behaviour. The way her sons' differences corresponded to differences between her husband and her led to look for their more biologically based sources. This turned out to be her in the area of temperament.

Rothbart defined temperament as individual differences in reactivity and self-regulation (Rothbart & Bates, 1998, 2006; Rothbart & Derryberry, 1981). Reactivity also refers to the orienting of attention to internal and external stimulation. Temperamental reactivity is seen in broad tendencies, such as negative reactivity or distress proneness, and it is also seen in more specific reactions, such as tendencies to fear or anger, and aspects of physiological reactivity, such as heart rate or galvanic skin response. Self-regulatory aspects of temperament serve to act upon reactive tendencies, increasing or moderating them. Self-regulation includes individual differences in effortful control operating through attention. Effortful control can serve to decrease or increase the onset, intensity, or duration of temperament reactions (Rothbart, 2011).

According to Rothbart, Children's temperament responses are along thus likely to impact their mental models of individuals (as approachable or risky), and of the self (as lovable or unlovable). The impact of temperament on these perspectives of the self as well as other people will be automatic and reflected essentially in the infant's behaviour, yet later it can be represented in explanations about the self and other individuals, moving more clearly into the area of personality (Rothbart, 2011).

CONCEPT OF TEMPERAMENT AND CHARACTER

Temperament is one of the dimensions of the personality. That is the influence of biological sides of the personality. The term temperament covers neuropsychological descriptions of the personality.

Temperament has strong connections of the neurobiology. The concept of temperament already traced back to nearly two thousand years ago when it is discovered by Hippocrates and Galen through their theory of humours in the body. Personality psychologist now clearly categorized into traits, temperament, and character, each has clear different feedbacks on personality.

Temperament refers to individual characteristic of emotional excitability or intensity that recognize the first two weeks after birth, where as traits are the dispositions of an individuals. These inherited traits are leads to the type of temperaments of an individual.

Temperament characteristics are shown in the new born and now a day also can be measurable in the fetus. The new born babies show their reactions about approach and avoidance of situations with smiling, crying, laughter and body movements also.

Many studies reveal that the newborn easily recognize their mother or caregivers and their physical approach is seen usually by 4 to 6 months. Anger or frustration is seen at 2 to 3 months and fear in the form of behavioural inhibition appears to be differentiated from general distress proneness by 7 to 10 months. Fear in infancy predicts children's later fearfulness and low aggression; anger predicts later higher frustration and aggression. Fear thus appears to act as a control on both approach and aggression (Rothbart & Bates, 2006). Based on the evidences temperament should be relatively stable across life.

Historically, Hippocrates and Galen described four temperaments such as melancholic, phlegmatic, sanguine and choleric. These are the bodily fluids that determine ones nature of diseases. Based on these evidences of the four classical temperaments, many researchers stated their new innovations in the area of temperament traits.

Thomas and Chess's nine dimensions of temperament characteristics

- Activity level: This is the child's "idle speed or how active the child is generally.
- Rhythmicity (regularity): The trait refers to the predictability of biological functions like appetite and sleep.
- Approach or withdrawal: Refers to the child's characteristic response to a new situation or strangers.
- Adaptability: Related to how easily the child adapts to transitions and changes, like switching to a new activity.
- Sensory threshold: it is associatedto how the childrens are sensitive to physical stimuli. Sensory threshold is the amount of stimulation (sounds, tastes, touch, temperature changes)of sensory stimuli which is needed to produce a response in the child.
- Intensity of reaction: The energy level of a response whether positive or negative.

- Quality of mood: This is the tendency to react to the world primarily in a positive or negative way.
- Distractibility: The degree of interference of external stimuli to the concentration and paying attention displayed when a child is not particularly interested in an activity.
- Attention span and persistence: This is the length of time a child continues in activities in the face of obstacles.

Mary K.Rothbart's three dimensions of temperament characteristics are;

- Surgency, or extraversion: composed of scales such as positive anticipation, activity level, and sensation seeking
- Negative affectivity. including fear, anger frustration and social discomfort
- Effortful control: which includes facets such as inhibitory control, attentional focusing, and perceptual sensitivity

Cloninger's theories of temperament characteristics are;

Novelty seeking, harm avoidance, reward dependence, and persistence, which are independently heritable, manifest early in life, and involve preconceptual biases in perceptual memory and habit formation.

(I) Novelty seeking (NS)
1. Exploratory excitability (NS1)
2. Impulsiveness (NS2)
3. Extravagance (NS3)
4. Disorderliness (NS4)

(II) Harm avoidance (HA)
1. Anticipatory worry (HA1)
2. Fear of uncertainty (HA2)
3. Shyness (HA3)
4. Fatigability (HA4)

(III) Reward dependence (RD)
1. Sentimentality (RD1)
2. Openness to warm communication (RD2)
3. Attachment (RD3)
4. Dependence (RD4)

(IV) Persistence (PS)
1. Eagerness of effort (PS1)
2. Work hardened (PS2)
3. Ambitious (PS3)
4. Perfectionist (PS4)

Cloninger was realized that his theory of temperament profile do not differentiate between the clinical and non clinical populations. Thus, he added character through the help of cognitive, social development research, according to humanistic personality theories and transpersonal psychology, hence the three dimensions of character resulted, that are; self-directedness, co-cooperativeness and self-transcendence (Gillespie *et.al.*, 2003).

Character refers to individual differences in goals, values and self conscious emotions like shame, guilt and empathy that are expressed by the association of a person with him or herself, with other people, with group of people, with society and within the universe.Character is characterized to reflect individual differences in self-concept according the degree of identification with him/herself as self-sufficient individual, with other individuals and with the entire universe (Brändström, 2009). The character dimensions depict how an individual identifies with themselves, other individuals and different objects (Cloninger and Svrakic, 1997). Contingent upon the self-concept an individual has, it will adjust the meaning of what the individual experiences, and accordingly the individual's emotional response will likewise be changed (Brändström, 2009). Therefore, the character dimensions are seen as having aintellectual aspects about self/non-self limits and also a emotional aspect (Cloninger *et al.*, 1994).

While it was at first trusted that character aspects are represented traits that are weakly acquired and moderately influenced by social learning, later it was found that they were as inheritable as temperament traits, despite the fact that they contrasted from temperament in that they expressedan individual'sgoals and values, as opposed to their emotional style (Cloninger, 2004). In the long run Cloninger recommended that temperament was an indication of the working of the brain's habit systems (associative learning) whereas character was a manifestation of the brain's semantic learning of facts and propositions. Character aspects can achieve different levels of maturity in a stepwise pattern. Dependent to the related area the character aspects are characterized as Self-Directedness (SD), Cooperativeness (CO) and Self-Transcendence (ST) (Brändström, 2009).

According to Cloninger *et al.* (1994) individuals high on the SD dimensionare said to be "mature, strong, self-sufficient, responsible, reliable, goal-orientated, constructive, and well-integrated individuals when they have the opportunity for personal leadership". Individuals low on the SD dimension, on the other hand, are said to be "immature, weak, fragile, blaming, destructive, ineffective, irresponsible, unreliable, and poorly integrated when they are not conforming to the direction of a mature leader" (Dennison, 2012).

ST associates to the extent to which individuals consider themselves an important part inthe universe. It is reflected in spiritually mature, unpretentious, humble, and fulfilled individuals. Individuals high on the ST dimension are said to be "unpretentious, fulfilled, patient, creative, selfless, and spiritual" (Cloninger *et al.*, 1994). Onthe contrary, individuals who are low on the ST dimension are said to be "proud, impatient, unimaginative, and unappreciative of art, self-aware, materialistic, andunfulfilled" (Dennison, 2012).

Finally, character dimension of CO, which relates to the extent to which individuals consider themselves an important part in society. It is reflected in socially mature, empathic, agreeable and cooperative individuals. Individuals high on the CO dimension are said to be "empathetic, tolerant, compassionate, supportive, fair, andprincipled individuals" (Cloninger *et al.*, 1994). Individuals low on the dimensionof CO, in comparison are said to be "self-absorbed, intolerant, critical, unhelpful, revengeful, and opportunistic" (Dennison, 2012).

Neural Correlates of Temperament

Neuro-imaging researches identified that activates brain net works underlying temperament. Temperament has been related to neural structure, especially to the functioning of amygdale and dopamine systems.

As noted earlier, there is a long history regarding the physiological bases of individual differences in temperament, described by the Hippocrates – Galen typology of four humours. Centuries later, Pavlov and colleagues were presented clearly foreshadowed current trends in the study of neural bases of temperament and personality. That is; his theoretical models detailed to relating the strength or integrity of central nervous system (CNS) to individual differences in motivation and emotion. His model provided the evidences of the CNS processes and its interplay between the excitatory versus inhibitory process. Therefore Pavlov's general model provided the foundation for the biological bases of temperament. The gradual development of the neural circuitry underlying effortful control and it is associated with the executive functions with emerging self regulatory skills, open up a particularly exciting area of future research in the study of temperament. Normative developmental changes in effortful control processing and underlying neural systems, allows for the study of the effects of genes, experience and experiences on the emergence of self regulatory processes at both biological and behavioural level of analysis (Henderson & Wachs, 2007).

According to the approach of Rothbart, an important assumption in his model is that both reactive and self regulatory behaviours are intimately linked to the neurobiological process (Zentner & Bates, 2008). Unlike Rothbart's theory, Kagan's bio-typological approach to the study of temperament is more inductive. Kagan and colleagues studied longitudinal study of behavioral inhibition and its counterpart of behavioural and physiological manifestations from early infancy onward.

Cloninger clearly describes the connections between characteristics of temperament and neurotransmitter systems. Specifically, he see novelty seeking, the tendency to seek out novel stimulations as influenced by the dopaminergetic system; harm avoidance, the tendency to avoid aversive stimulations and show behavioural inhibition, as impacted by the serotonergic system, and reward dependence, the tendency to search out and strongly respond to social rewards, as an expression of the neuroadrenergic system. Persistence, the tendency to be persevering and industrious has not been attributed to a particularneurotransmitter system (Cloninger, 1987).

Along with the other reviews of temperament shows that it has strong pillars, including gender, neurobiological substrates, endophenotypes and overt behaviour patterns. Increasing evidence that the biological makeup of children can be altered by early and even prenatal experiences (Huizink, 2008) should this differentiating between inherited and acquired components of temperament? These are the complex issues that will be challenging to the future research works.

Henderson & Wachs (2007) believed that it is essential to study the development of temperament and the neural processes underlying reactivity and self regulation across infancy, childhood and adolescence. They had given only modest levels of stability in assessments of temperament across time and the protracted developmental course of many neural structures underlying self regulation. The effects of bio-ecological and psycho social factors on temperament related CNS functioning also is there. Studying these processes at any given point in development will only provide a snapshot of cognition- emotion interactions underlying social development. Henderson & Wachs are incorporating longitudinal assessments of both behaviour and neural functioning.

Temperament as a Risk Factor in Social and Academic Development

Temperament is originated at the time of newborn and also it has strong connections of neural correlates. Hence it has been developing through the child's development with the help of environmental feedbacks and neural basis of substrates. It is consistently related to important social behaviours such as empathy and conscience.

The relation between temperament and conscience was also affected by parenting. Temperament related behaviour and parenting behaviour also influence child's socio-emotional development, both are independently associated with the other. More studies reported that there is a connection between children, emotional reactivity and parenting. That is child fearfulness and emotional regulation, predicts more parental warmth and more positive control. Hence low levels of parental warmth predict increases in fearfulness and negative emotional regulations. Similarly, parental warmth predicts better child self regulations, and more negative parental control predicts poorer child self regulations. Among these evidences, parenting may play an important role in moderating the outcomes of child's temperament. Also research suggests the importance of education to help child care workers, teachers and parents realize that children's behaviour and emotions are not solely the result of social learning. Shy children have to benefit from being encouraged by overprotecting parents, hence the child remain shy and inhibited to explore novel situations, where as more restrictive controlled and lower parental negativity results child's aggressive and difficult to manage behaviours.

An association between children's temperament characteristics and academic achievement has been found. In Martin's model, temperament is one of factors that functions across home and school setting and affects learning and school behaviour. Children's classroom behaviour affects peers attitudes towardshis behaviour, which in turn have an additional important on the child's educational outcome. These peers attitude and behaviour toward a learner identified as emotionally/behaviourally disordered may have additional impact because of the increases risk for social rejection (https://www.education.com/reference/article/temperament-emotional-behavioral-disorders).

Temperamental risk is not static since adapting resources that moderate vulnerability keep on growing with maturation and experience (Stuss, 1992). The connections have been shows between temperament and deficits in social competence, between temperament and academic achievement, and between LD and deficits in social competence (Teglasi, Cohn & Meshbesher, 2004). Temperament may amplify difficulties with processing information, and thus contribute to being identified with LD, and difficulties with information processing make it harder to deal with the challenges of adverse temperamental dispositions. Considering the connection between children'sdaily functioning and their academic progress (Welsh, Parke, Widaman, & O'Neil, 2001), it is not surprising that school-based interventions that effectively implies children's social and emotional needs also improve academic performance (Graczyk *et al.*, 2000).

Generally, high distractible and low persistence are associated with low academic performances. Temperament may amplify difficulties with processing information, because it has also a connection between the attention and motivation. Inhibited children have a slightly greater chance than other children's of developing anxiety or depression; therefore they have difficulties in academic competencies. Easygoing children are successfully overcome these competencies. Another thing is that children's interpret the environmental experiences differently depends upon their nature of temperament. That is irritable or anxious children easily tend to perceive negative outcomes in their school, family or surroundings. Although they become easily depressed.

All individual are different to the other. Throughout history, psychologist and researchers have tried to quantify personality and as its result, numerous theories are emerging in the area of personality now itself. Temperament is the important factor of personality. It has wide influence in the life of an individual, because it also develops at the birth of a child. That's why many researchers interested to found its newer facts and influences on personality, and it has greater impact on socialization. Children temperament shapes their outcomes of life. Parents and teachers have relevant role to maintain or built efficient temperament of a child, other than the genetical impact of their temperament. Inherited traits and parenting are the risk factors for social and academic development.The link between learning problems and social-emotional difficulties is well documented and both are associated with temperamental risk factors. Likewise temperament factors are made conflicts to the academic performance of children. It can be manageable in certain level with the help of teachers and parents.

The Foundations of Character

The three character dimensions of personality - SD, CO and ST - depend on social and cognitive development (Bond, 2001) and involve individual differences in self concepts about goals and values (Cloninger *et al.*, 1994). Self-concepts vary in connection to the degree to which an individual perceives themselves as (1) an autonomous individual (SD), (2) a vital part of mankind (C), and (3) a vital part of the universe all in all (ST) (Cloninger *et al.*, 1993).

The character dimensions start to create in earliest stages with newborn child parental attachment, at that point in self separation in toddlers, and proceed to develop and mature all through life (Cloninger and Svrakic, 1997). In this manner, the character dimensions mature in adulthood and ultimately impacts individual and social effectiveness (Cloninger *et al.*, 1993). Character attributes that are ineffectively developed can be connected to all categorical subtypes of personality disorders and can be used to analyze the presence and the severity of personality disorder.

The character dimensions include individual differences in higher cognitive functions (Svrakic *et al.*, 2002), for example, self-concepts about goals and values. Character is accepted to be environmentally influenced, dependent on an individual's experiences, impacted by social and culturalinfluences and has been related with various psychotherapeutic methodologies (Prosnick *et al.*, 2003). Along these, character is a acquired part of personality and as indicated by Mardaga and Hansenne (2007) character isn't identified with innate and neurobiological underpinnings. Clashing to this Cloninger *et al.* (1994) recommend that neuroanatomy influences character, to such an extent that prefrontal activity is anticipated to be predominantly essential for SD, the tempo-parietal activity is anticipated to be overwhelmingly basic for the CO and the unity of action in homologous sections of the two sides of the brain is anticipated to be predominantly essential for the ST.

EXECUTIVE FUNCTIONS OF FRONTAL LOBE

Executive function was first described as a "central executive" by Baddeley and Hitch (1974) and later defined by Lezak (1983) as the dimension of human behaviour that deals with "how" behaviour is expressed. Executive functions were conceptualized as having four components: The abilities of goal orientation, planning, and effective performance. Lezak added that these behaviours are all necessary for suitable, socially responsible and effectively self-serving adult conduct. Since executive functions are perfect, a person who has sustained considerable cognitive loss can still continue to be independent and productive.

Executive functions help novel problem solving and modification of behaviour because of changes in the environment. It helps in planning and formulating strategies for complex activities and the capacity to inhibit adverse behaviour and emotional responses to participate in goal directed behaviour (Williams *et al.*, 2009). In this way, executive functioning is made out of behavioural, affective, motivational and cognitive components (Alvarez and Emory, 2006; Suchy, 2009).

Duncan *et al.* (1996), for instance, suggest that goal neglect is a common mechanism characterizing the nature of deficits present in frontal lobe patients, and that this neglect is highly linked to Spearman's factor. These and other authors believe in the existence of a unifying, central factor (i.e., general intelligence or working memory) underlying executive functioning and the organization of goal-directed behaviour (Duncan *et al.* 1996; De Frias *et al*, 2006; Parkin and Java, 1999; Kimberg *et al.* 1997).

Historically, executive functions have been connected to the prefrontal cortex of the brain, and keep on being so today. This conviction emerged from studies that showed that people who performed ineffectively on test of abstract reasoning and verbal fluency had severe injuries in their frontal lobe. However, such studies have additionally been observed to be inconsistent. It is not necessarily the say that executive functions are not connected to the frontal lobe, but instead the frontal projections may take part in a more prominent degree than different areas of the brain in functions thought to be "executive" (Alvarez and Emory, 2006; Suchy, 2009).

There is additionally a verbal confrontation with respect to how best to assess executive functioning. Well known and commonly utilized measures that have been used to assess executive functioning include the Wisconsin Card Sorting Test (WCST), Phonemic Verbal Fluency, Trail Making, Stroop Color Word Interference Test and Digit Symbol (Alvarez and Emory, 2006; Salt house, 2005).

One of the best methods of measuring executive function is The Wisconsin Card Sorting Test (WCST). The WCST was originally developed to assess abstract reasoning ability and the ability to shift cognitive strategies in response to changing environmental contingencies (Berg, 1948; Grant & Berg, 1948). As such, the WCST can be considered a measure of 'executive function', consisting the ability to develop and maintain an appropriate problem solving strategy across changing stimulus conditions in order to achieve a future goal (Luria, 1973). Similar to other measures of executive function, the WCST measures organized searching, strategic planning, utilizing environmental feedback to shift cognitive sets, modulating impulsive responding and directing behaviour toward achieving a goal, (Chelune & Baer, 1986; Gnys & Willis, 1991; Perrine, in press).

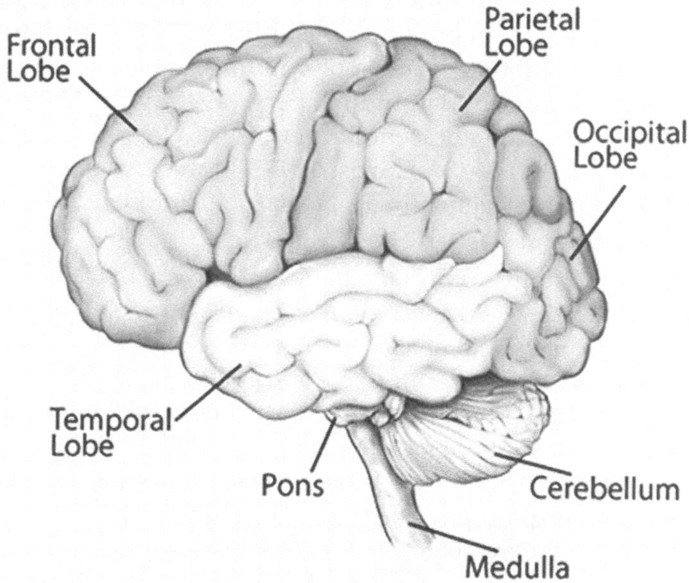

Fig. 2.3: The structure of the brain

Studies of Executive Functions of Frontal Lobe

A study results by Salthouse (2005) set about to investigate the relationship between cognitive processes and various variables that have been used to show executive functioning. This study found that there was a strong relationship between measures of executive functioning and the cognitive processes of reasoning and perceptual speed abilities. However, in a study by Alverez and Emory (2006) they used the Wisconsin Card Sorting Test, Phonemic Verbal Fluency and Stroop Color Word Interference Test to authenticate the method of linking executive functioning to frontal lobe lesions. This study did not find a "one-to-one relationship between executive functions and frontal lobe activity". They conclude the frontal lobes as well as the regions in the other lobes of the brain are required for effective executive functions (Dennison, 2012).

In the custom of testing thinking processes or mental set, in 1900, Ach built up the sorting task in which subjects needed to sort cards with non-sense words in view of regular highlights shared by the objects the words represented. Afterward, in 1920, Goldstein reported the use of sorting tasks to test concrete and abstract attitudes in brain-damaged patients. Following Ach and Goldstein, the Wisconsin Card Sorting Test (WCST) was devised in 1948 by Grant and Berg as an index of abstract reasoning, concept formation, and response strategies to changing contextual contingencies (Eling, Derckx & Maes, 2008). Years later, Milner, a neuropsychologist at the Neurological Institute of Montreal, acquainted the WCST to assess prefrontal lobe dysfunctions in patients with brain injuries (Milner, 1963). At present, there are no less than two different systems of administration and scoring of the WCST; the standard form by Grant and Berg (1948) with Milner´s (1963) correction criteria and the shortened version by Heaton (Heaton, 1981; Heaton, Chelune, Talley, Kay, & Curtis, 1993). Moreover, the test has been administered in modified versions by Nelson (1976), Delis, Squire, Bihrle and Massman (1992) and Barceló (1999, 2001).

Several classic studies reported the sensitivity of the WCST tofrontal lobe lesions (Drewe, 1974; Milner, 1963; Nelson, 1976; Robinson, Heaton, Lehman, & Stilson, 1980; Teuber, Battersby & Bender, 1951). Many authors have later questioned the sensitivity and specificity of the WCST to frontal lobe lesion or dysfunction in neurological or psychiatric patients, respectively. Consequently, some handbooks of neuropsychological assessment advise aboutthe risk of using WCST scores as a direct marker of frontal lobedamage without other converging evidence (Lezak, Howieson, & Loring, 2004; Strauss, Sherman & Spreen, 2006)

Recently, many clinical studies of WCST performance report impairment on the WCST with frontal cortex damage (Demakis, 2003; Freedman, Black, Ebert, & Binns, 1998; Giovagnoli, 2001; Goldstein, Obrzut, John, Ledakis, & Armstrong, 2004; Igarashi *et al.*, 2002; Leskela *et al.*, 1999; Mukhopadhyay *et al.*, 2008; Nelson, 1976; Robinson *et al.*, 1980; Stuss *et al.*, 2000).

In spite of the fact that there have been reports of left frontal damage influencing WCST performance more than right frontal damage (Goldstein *et al.*, 2004), others report no difference in laterality of damage in the frontal cortex (Demakis, 2003; Giovagnoli, 2001). Moreover, many clinical studies show that damage in non-frontal (Leskela *et al.*, 1999; van den Broek, Bradshaw & Szabadi, 1993) or diffuse damage in frontal and non-frontal regions (Axelrod *et al.*, 1996; Anderson, Damasio, Jones & Tranel, 1991;) both affect WCST performance. More specifically, many authors have reported that damage to temporal (Corcoran & Upton, 1993; Giovagnoli, 2001; Hermann, Wyler & Richey, 1988; Horner, Flashman, Freides, Epstein & Bakay, 1996; Strauss, Hunter & Wada, 1993), subcortical (Mukhopadhyay *et al.*, 2008), hippocampal (Corcoran & Upton, 1993; Giovagnoli, 2001; Igarashi *et al.*, 2002), and even cerebellar regions (Mukhopadhyay *et al.*, 2008) cause similar impairments on WCST performance as those subsequent to frontal lobe lesions.

Current models of central executive functions perceive that cognitive control includes a system of brain structures that are not only localized to the frontal lobes (Baddeley, 2002). Also, it has been demonstrated that patients with frontal damage regularly don't indicate executive deficits, though patients without frontal damage frequently presentexecutive deficits (Andres, 2003; Baddeley & Wilson, 1988).

Many studies provides evidence of impaired sub-domains of executive functions (i.e., mental shifting, flexibility) in children with Developmental Coordination Disorder (DCD). They studied Seventy-one children with DCD and 70 children without motor problems were recruited from 14 public schools. Executive functions and school functions were assessed using the WCST, and the School Function Assessment – Chinese Version (SFA-C) respectively.In their studies also found the logistic regression analysis showed differences between two groups on eight SFA-C subscales, and significant correlation between items measured on WCST and SFA-C.

Theories of Executive Function

Various influential models and theories of executive function have been proposed in an effort to integrate the control processes of the frontal lobe into a coherent framework. Baddeley and Hitch (1974) proposed a model of working memory that included a phonological loop, a visuo-spatial sketchpad and a central executive responsible for the control and regulation of cognitive processes (Baddeley 2002), such as planning and organization of information (Hobson and Leeds 2001). The phonological system includes a phonological store that is able to hold information for about two seconds and an articulatory loop which maintains the information through rehearsal (Baddeley 1986, 1992). The central executive, on the other hand, is a system of attentional control able to focus and switch attention, but without a storage capacity (Baddeley and Logie 1999). Working memory processes have been known to be mediated by the prefrontal cortex (Eldreth *et al.* 2006) with the DL prefrontal areas being engaged the most during mental manipulation of information (D'Esposito *et al.* 1999).

The idea of a "central" executive is sometimes understood as proposing a homuncular nature of executive functioning (Zelazo and Muller 2002), but according to Baddeley (1998) this component of working memory does not reject the possibility of a fractionality of the executive with sub processes that could be (and have been) mapped anatomically (Baddeley, 2002).

Another important model in the literature is that of Norman and Shallice (1986), which describes the control of information processing. Their model includes a Supervisory Attentional System (SAS) necessary for situations in which planning for future actions, making decisions and working with novel stimuli are required. A central aspect of this model is the distinction between automatic (routine) and controlled (non-routine) processes.

Stuss and Alexander (2000), for instance, agree with the notion of a SAS made up of distinct parts but question the adequacy of a two-level model (controlled versus automatic) in favor of an idea of multiple levels of control. Zelazo *et al*. (1997) have taken an alternative approach to the study of executive function, appropriate by Luria's concept of "interactive functional systems" (Luria 1973) and they form a concept, it as a complex function, or macrostructure, with executive sub functions that work together to accomplish the higher-order function of solving problems. Four temporally and functionally distinct phases of problem solving are identified which correspond to different aspects of executive processing: problem representation, planning, execution, and evaluation. The major advantage of this framework is that not only does the outcome of executive functions become evident (i.e., solving the problem or not) but it also allows locating failures of executive functioning in a temporal sequence of problem solving (Zelazo *et al*. 1997). Complex functions such as those of the executive, according to Zelazo and Muller (2002), cannot be represented exclusively in the prefrontal areas, but need to the integrity of other brain areas as well. Zelazo *et al*. (1997) reject the approach of the uniqueness of the frontal lobe in the control of executive functions.

The study of the neural correlates of executive functioning stems from earlier observations of patients with frontal lesions. Soldiers wounded in war exhibited altered behaviour as well as an impaired ability to engage in appropriate actions toward the completion of a goal (Stuss and Benson 1986). Other patients with frontal lesions demonstrated difficulties in self-control and in attentional shifting (Golberg 2001; Lezak *et al*. 2004). The group of behavioural and cognitive anomalies found in frontal patients became known as the "dysexecutive syndrome" (Baddeley and Wilson 1988) which includes problems in planning, organization, abstraction reasoning, problem-solving, and decision-making (Ardila and Surloff 2004; Norris and Tate 2000; Hobson and Leeds 2001). Although early observations suggested a homogenous involvement of the frontal lobes, and mainly the prefrontal cortex, executive functions are now accepted to be associated with different regions of the frontal lobes (Stuss and Alexander 2000; Stuss *et al*. 2002; Koechlin *et al*. 2000) as well as distributed over a wide cerebral network which includes subcortical structures and thalamic pathways (Monchi *et al*. 2006; Kassubek *et al*. 2005). Both the frontal and posterior associative cortices (Collette and van der Linden 2002) have been suggested to mediate functions of the executive system. Wager and Smith (2003) demonstrated in a recent meta-analysis that different executive processes are associated with specific cerebral areas.

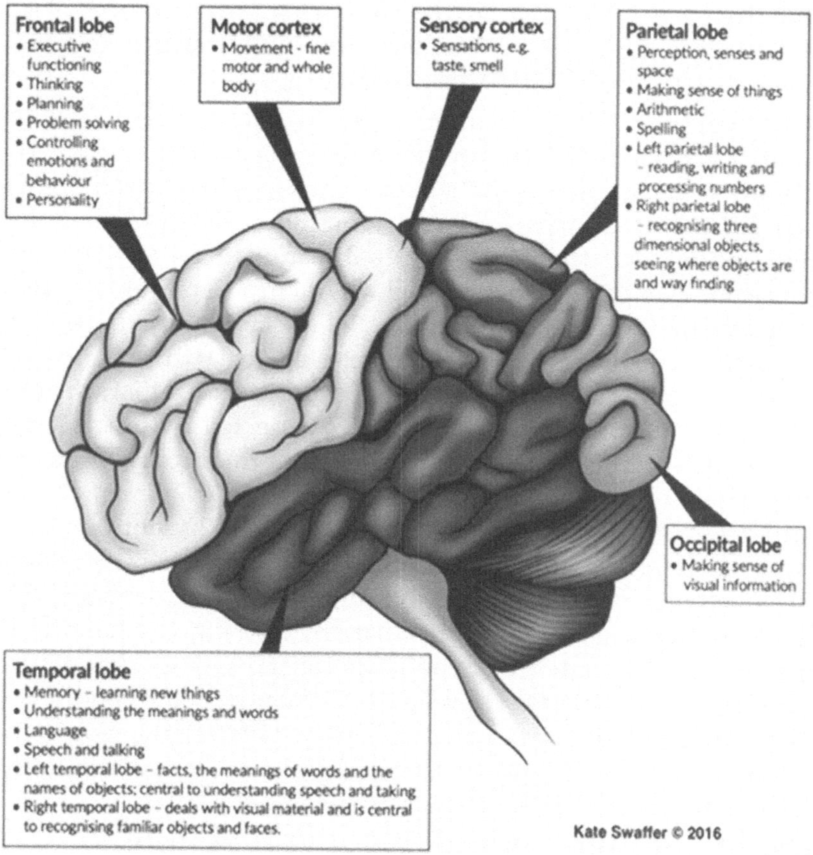

Fig. 2.4: The functions of the brain Neuroimaging Studies

In a recent review, Royall *et al.* (2002) stressed the importance of neural circuits comprising the frontal lobes, the basal ganglia and the thalamus for performance on executive tests. Collette *et al.* (2005) using positron emission tomography (PET) found that common areas of the brain are activated by three different executive functions (updating, shifting, and inhibition). These regions included the posterior regions of the left superior parietal gyrus and the right intraparietal sulcus.

Most neuroimaging studies on WCST performance report a significant increase in metabolic or neural activity within frontal or prefrontal cortical regions (Barceló & Knight, 2002; Barceló *et al.*, 2006; Berman *et al.*, 1995; Catafau *et al.*, 1994, 1998; Cicek & Nalcaci, 2001; Gonzalez-Hernandez *et al.*, 2002, 2003; Kawasaki *et al.*, 1993; Konishi *et al.*, 1998, 2002; Konishi, Asari, Jimura & Miyashita, 2003; Lie, Specht, Marshall & Fink, 2006; Lombardi *et al.*, 1999; Marenco, Daniel, Coppola Zigun & Weinberger, 1993; Mentzel *et al.*, 1998; Monchi, Petrides, Petre, Worsley & Dagher, 2001; Parellada *et al.*,

1998; Ragland *et al.*, 1998; Tien, Schlaepfer, Orr & Pearlson, 1998; Nagahama *et al.*, 1996, 1997, 1998; Rogers, Grasby, Brooks, Andrews & Robbins, 2000; Volz *et al.*, 1997; Wang, Kakigi & Hoshiyama, 2001).

Goldberg *et al.* (1987) studied a group of chronically hospitalized schizophrenia patients. In one condition the patients were informed of the underlying sorting principles of the WCST at the beginning of the test (color, form, and number). In the second condition the authors provided the same sorting principles on a trial-by-trial basis. The authors found that only when the instructions were given trial-by-trial was there a significant improvement from baseline performance. Furthermore, when the trial-by-trial instructions were discontinued and the patients were retested, their performance returned to their impaired baseline levels. Goldberg *et al.* concluded that schizophrenia patients' poor performance on the WCST reflected a "trait phenomena consistent with a failure of cognitive processes traditionally attributed to the prefrontal cortex" (Goldberg *et al.*, 1987, p. 1003). Green *et al.* (1992) conducted a study on 46 schizophrenic patients and 20 control participants who were each serially administered the WCST under four conditions that varied monetary reinforcement and level of instruction. Essentially, the brain can learn to bypass neural pathways that not working and build new ones not just in childhood, but through adolescence and even adulthood (Doidge, 2007; Greenstone, 2011). British researches Blakemore and Choudhury (2006) speculated that these findings point to "a period of synaptic reorganisation" when adolescent brains might be particularly responsive to efforts to regulate executive functions and social cognition (Greenstone, 2011).

TEMPERAMENT, CHARACTER AND EXECUTIVE FUNCTIONS

The connection between temperament and character and executive functions has not been explored enough. It has been hypothesized that both temperament and character dimensions share a typical fundamental neural base with several executive functioningtasks (Bergvall *et al.*, 2003). Be that as it may, there is a scarcity of studies dealing with this links, especially in non-clinical examples (Cassimjee and Murphy, 2010).

As indicated by Bergvall *et al.* (2003) numerous executive functions and temperament dimensions include the prefrontal cortex. The prefrontal cortex and its other related cortical regions are included with planning, abstraction, attention and working memory tasks, which can be classified under executive functioning (Cassimjee and Murphy, 2010). Therefore, executive functioning is crucial for everyday human behaviour, which is the reason for deficits in executive functions have been pinpointed as an essential factor in different mental disorders (Henderson and Wachs, 2007).

There is a developing widespread conviction that there is a significant relationship between temperament and the particular psychopathologies. Cloninger's psychobiological model and his TCI can evaluate the presence and severity of personality disorders and is now frequently utilized as a part of clinical studies that examine the link between personality and different psychopathologies. Putatively individual differences in temperament and character affect the risk of different psychopathologies (Cloninger and Svrakic, 1997). A couple of clinical investigations that have discovered a significant connection between temperament, character and psychopathologies will be discussed.

Bergvall *et al.* (2003) investigated the connection between personality change and deficiencies in cognitive executive functions in offenders. The study was tried to relate personality and executive functioning originated from two observations. Firstly, similar ideas, for example, "impulsivity" have been utilized as a part of both executive functions undertakings and in dimensions of personality. Another one is that different executive functions and personality dimensions include the prefrontal cortex. This originates from various research examines (Miller, 2000; Roberts, Robins and Weiskrantz, 1996; Smith and Jonides, 1999) that have connected the prefrontal cortex with working memory, planning, attention, inhibition and set-shifting. They found a significant relationship between character and execution on a set-shifting task (executive function). This could be clarified on the premise that character dimension on the TCI expand on complex psychological procedures including insight learning and reorganization of experience (Bergvall *et al.*, 2003).

Boeker *et al.* (2006) in their exploratory research investigated the relationship between neuropsychological functions, numerous dimensions on personality, and the different types of psychopathological symptoms. They found that the character dimensions of ST and SD were significantly related with working memory tasks in healthy individuals and were significantly associated with executive functioning tasks in schizophrenic individuals (Dennison, 2012).

A study done by Faraone, Kunwar, Adamson and Biederman (2009) investigated the relationship between adult ADHD and personality (utilizing the TCI). They found that individuals with ADHD had significant deviations on all TCI dimensions apart from RD and ST. Low scores on the P dimension is particularly relevant to this study as low P is consistent with the executive functioning deficit seen in a lot of individuals with ADHD. According to Anckarsäter *et al.* (2006) the existence of a personality disorder can be linked to character immaturity, which can be seen by low scores on Cloninger's character dimensions of SD and/or C. In their study they found that individuals with ADHD scored high on NS and HA dimensions (Dennison, 2012).

Drechsler *et al.*(2015) studied the relations between temperament, character, and executive functions in children with ADHD and clinical controls they found that there is a consistent overlap between Cloninger's temperament and character dimensions, and executive functions components as assessed by the BRIEF according to parent ratings. Behavioural aspects of self-regulation as well as cognitive aspects,which may be linked to the temperament dimensions of Novelty Seeking and Persistence, respectively.

In spite of the fact that Cloninger's psychobiological model shows the association between temperament dimensions to various basic neurotransmitter systems, it doesn't specifically identify with neuropsychological functioning. Interestingly, the temperament display by Rothbart and associates refers to executive control inclinations (Rothbart and Bates, 1998; Rothbart, Ellis, and Posner, 2004), which cover with Posner's neuropsychological idea of executive attention (Posner and Raichle, 1996).

Cassimjee and Murphy (2010) in a pilot study of temperament and character correlates of neuropsychological performance. They found that the computerised executive battery comprised a small select group of tests that measure specific aspects of executive functioning and abstract reasoning. They proposed that wider selection of tests tapping into different executive abilities may help in further understanding the relationships between specific temperament and character dimensions and executive functioning both in clinical and non-clinical groups. They also found that neuropsychological test performance is mediated by psychosocial factors and studies on larger samples with more diverse socio-demographics (age, gender, education and language) may further enhance understanding of the relationship between temperament, character and neuropsychological performance.

Conway and Stifter (2012) were to examine collaborations between child temperament and maternal behaviour in the prediction of child executive functions. Three types of temperament, such as inhibited, exuberant, and low reactive and two types of maternal behaviours during problem-solving, namely attention maintaining and attention redirection, were assessed at 2 years old in the laboratory.Maternal attention maintaining to verbal and non-verbal behaviour that helps child attention for maintain the focus on the task, while maternal attention diverting behaviours with respect to behaviours that redirect child attention away from the task. Results recommended that maternal attention-maintaining behaviours anticipated more higher levels of conflicts in executive functions, however just for inhibited and exuberant children. Maternal consideration redirection anticipated poorer impulse control and conflict executive functions, yet just for inhibited children.

In a recent study found that children with more difficult temperaments may be more susceptible to maternal behaviours than children with less difficult temperaments, but only regarding the development of impulse control abilities. There was no clear evidence of such moderation for conflict executive function. These results support the idea that distinct mechanisms may underlie the development of different dimensions of child executive functions (Rochette & Bernier, 2016).

CONCLUSION

From the above mentioned studies clearly shows that there is a clear connections in temperament, character and executive functions. Each of these has a neural correlates of back up. The temperament, character and executive functions also have a strong impact of academic, social and everyday life situations. In the light of some of these available theoretical and empirical literature gives the courage to the present study.

3

Methods

"It is important to get results from experiment but the most important is the process in getting that results".

–Dr. Nik Ahmad Nizam

INTRODUCTION

The aim of the present study is to find out the temperament, character and executive functions among Students with and without Learning Disabilities. The study evolved two phases. In the first phase, the expert team was validated the instrument and conducted pilot study to the instrument and finally, in the second phase, was to study the objectives of the study.

RESEARCH DESIGN

Research design is a plan or strategy for conducting the research. Research designs are specific to the type of research. A research design is a more general plan and that a single design may contain and require the use of several methods. In order to achieve the objectives of the study the investigator selected the descriptive method. Three main purposes of research are to describe, explain, and validate findings. Description emerges following creative exploration, and serves to organize the findings in order to fit them with explanations, and then test or validate those explanations (Krathwohl, 1993). Descriptive research involves gathering data that describe events and then organizes, tabulates, depicts, and describes the data collection (Glass & Hopkins, 1984). Among the distinct approaches that may be used in descriptive research design, the semi structured interview was used for the present study.

PROCEDURE FOR DATA COLLECTION

The investigator contacted the school authorities with the letter of introduction of School of Behavioral Sciences. The scope of the study was explained to them and permission was sought for collecting data from students.

After getting the permission from the school authorities, the investigator initially fill the personal data sheet through the Students with and without Learning Disabilities. After establishing proper rapport, the investigator administered the instruments the Students with and without Learning Disabilities after the screening by using IQ test and learning disabilities screening tests.

The instrument used for the present study are, a general data sheet, Wisconsin Card Sorting Test (WCST) and the Early Adolescent Temperament and Character Inventory (EATCI). The general data sheet includes details of the student such as name, gender, age, class and the school

PHASE 1

In phase 1, in order to achieve the objectives of the study the investigator developed the instrument and standardized. As the initial stage of the research, the researcher had done a pilot study.

SAMPLING PROCEDURE

Selection of a sample is very important step in conducting any research study. The quality of sample determines the possibility for generalization. From the different sampling techniques, the investigator selected random sampling procedures for the selection of the sample of Students with and without Learning Disabilities used for the standardization of the study.

SAMPLE

200 samples including Students with Learning Disabilities and Students without Learning Disabilities were selected for pilot study. Sample details are given below:

Table 3.1: The variables, group and frequency of the sample used for the pilot study

Sl.No.	Variables	Group	Frequency
1.	Group	With LD	60
		Without LD	140
2.	Age	13-14	105
		15-16	95
3.	Location	Kollam	73
		Pathanamthitta	56
		Kottayam	71

INSTRUMENTS

1. Personal data sheet prepared by the investigator to gather the socio demographic variables such as name, age, gender and class of the subjects.
2. The Early Adolescent Temperament Character Inventory (EATCI) self report.

Description of the Instrument

The instrument used for the present study are, a general data sheet and the Early Adolescent Temperament and Character Inventory (EATCI), prepared by the investigator. The general data sheen includes details of the student such as name, gender, age, class and the school.

The Early Adolescent Temperament and Character Inventory (EATCI) is a self report inventory which consists of 89 items and they were asked to put a tick mark on the forwarding response in the five point scale to find out the temperament and character of the adolescent group. Temperament consists of 4 dimensions with 12 sub dimensions and character consists of 3 dimensions only. Scoring will be discussing in the phase two sections.

RELIABILITY

After the pilot study, reliability was found in terms of the internal consistency. The item analyzed by the most common Cronbach alpha with the help of SPSS software version 16.

The instrument has 7 major domains and 15 sub domains, reliability statistics for each sub domains was estimated and its summary is given below. One thing to keep in mind in measuring internal consistency using Cronbach alpha is that if applied separately to each of these subscales (Field, 2012), as a rule of thumb, Cronbach alpha values of 0.7 and more spelled as quiet good (Gliem & Gliem, 2003, Anu, 2016).

Table 3.2: The summary of Domains, Items and Cronbach alpha of the Early Adolescent Temperament and Character Inventory (EATCI)

Temperament and Character	Domains	No. of Items	Cronbach Alpha
Effortful control	Attention	6	0.83
	Inhibitory control	3	0.68
	Activation control	5	0.75
	High intensity pleasure	4	0.66
Surgency	Fear	5	0.7
	Shy	4	0.77
	Frustration	6	0.85
Negative affect	Depressive mood	5	0.83
	Aggression	6	0.86
	Affiliation	4	0.65
Affiliativeness	Perceptual sensitivity	3	0.73
	Pleasure sensitivity	3	0.70
	Self directedness	11	0.71
Character	Cooperativeness	10	0.76
	Self transcendence	5	0.71

VALIDITY

A test may reliable even though it is not valid. Thus a test which is measuring a specific concept must definitely measure the same concept consistently. Face validity was established by peer review and respondent review. Content validity refers to the degree to which the instrument actually measures, or is specifically related to the traits for which it was designed. Thus this instrument had been established content validity by a team of experts in the field.

PHASE 2

Phase two describes the details of the data collection part of the research in order to find out the objectives of the study.

POPULATION

Regardless of the technique to be used in selecting a sample, the first step in sampling is definition of population, which is the group in which the researcher would like to generalize the results. Students with and without Learning Disabilities attending in various schools in Kerala are the population for the present study.

Samples taken from the different schools of Kollam, Pathanamthitta and Kottayam districts of Kerala of the age group 13 to 16.

SAMPLING PROCEDURE

Random sampling method is used for the present study. Random sampling is used to ensure that a sample is representative of the population and the information collected can be generalized.

THE SAMPLE

According to the nature of the defined problem, the appropriate sampling should be used for the good research. In the words of Gay (1990) "sampling is the process of selecting a number of individuals for a study in such a way that the individual represents the larger group from which they were selected."

From the different sampling techniques, the investigator selected consecutive sampling procedures for the selection of the sample of Students with and without Learning Disabilities for the present study.

The sample consisted of total 40 Students with Learning Disabilities and 40 without Learning Disabilities they are studying under class 10.The subjects were of the age group 13 years to 16. Individuals with mental retardation, physical disability, and neurological disorders were excluded for convenience of the study. The samples were selected after the screening by using IQ test and learning disabilities screening tests.

Table 3.3: The variables, group and frequency of the sample

Sl.No.	Variables	Group	Frequency
1.	Group	With LD	40
		Without LD	40
2.	Age	13-14	47
		15-16	33
3.	Location	Kollam	45
		Pathanamthitta	12
		Kottayam	23

INCLUSION CRITERIA

The sample was included as sample in the study if the subjects were selected after the screening by using IQ test and learning disabilities screening tests. Those Students with Learning Disabilities who secured average or above average Intelligence Quotient (IQ), and obtained the certificate of learning disabilities from government authorized clinical psychologist were included in the sample.

EXCLUSION CRITERIA

The students with learning disabilities were excluded from sample in the study if the Students without Learning Disabilities facing visual, hearing, intellectual challenges or other social, emotional, family problems were excluded. Students with Learning Disabilities having other disabilities, who have no certificate from the government officials and who are under medication were excluded. The subjects, who returned incomplete or improperly answered the inventory were also excluded from the research study.

INSTRUMENTS

1. Personal data sheet (prepared by the investigator).
2. The Early Adolescent Temperament Character Inventory (EATCI) (prepared by the investigator).
3. Wisconsin Card Sorting Test (WCST) (The WCST was written by David A.Grant and Esta A.Berg. The Professional Manual for the WCST was written by Robert K.Heaton, Gordon J. Chelune, Jack L. Talley, Gary G. Kay and Glenn Curtiss).

DESCRIPTION OF INSTRUMENTS

1. General Data Sheet

This is prepared to collect general information about the children with learning disability. This include information such as the child's name, gender, age, standard of class and the name of school etc., this data sheet filled by the researcher himself.

2. The Early Adolescent Temperament Character Inventory (EATCI)

The Early Adolescent Temperament and Character Inventory (EATCI) has prepared by the investigator.

The Early Adolescent Temperament and Character Inventory (EATCI) is a self report inventory which consists of 82 items and they were asked to put a tick mark on the forwarding response in the five point scale to find out the temperament and character of the adolescent group. Temperament consists of 4 dimensions with 12 sub dimensions and character consists of 3 dimensions only.

Scoring

The scoring of the scale was done both forwarding and reverse with respect to the items. The forwarding scoring of the EATCI is 5, 4, 3, 2, 1 become strongly agree, agree, no comments, disagree & strongly disagree and vice versa. The reverse scoring of the items are 7, 8, 12, 24, 25, 56, 57, 62, 63, 70 & 72. If an item is omitted, that item receives no numerical score. The temperament items of the inventory was 1- 54 and character was 55-82.

3. Wisconsin Card Sorting Test (WCST)

The Wisconsin Cart Sorting Test (WCST; Heaton, Chelune, Talley, Kay & Curtiss, 1993) is a well-established measure of executive function. It is a neuropsychological assessment instrument, widely used for assessing higher-order cognitive functions that are related to the brain's frontal lobes. Successful completion of the WCST requires multiple cognitive operations, which include strategic planning, organized searching, the application of external feedback to shift mental sets, and the inhibition of impulsive responses. (Heaton, Chelune, Talley, Kay, Curtiss, 1993). These higher-order cognitive functions are called executive functions, and failure on the WCST performance implies executive dysfunction. The WCST was written by David A. Grant and Esta A. Berg. The Professional Manual for the WCST was written by Robert K. Heaton, Gordon J. Chelune, Jack L. Talley, Gary G. Kay and Glenn Curtiss. The test can be administered to those from 6.5 years to 89 years of age.

The WCST has 128-cards, and the WCST was administered according to instructions described in the WCST manual. The WCST consists of 4 stimulus cards and 2 identical decks of 64 response cards (a total of 128 response cards) (Heaton, Chelune, Talley, Kay, Curtiss, 1993). The response cards display figures of varying forms (crosses, circles, triangles, or stars), colors (red, blue, yellow, or green) and numbers of figures (Heaton, Chelune, Talley, Kay, Curtiss, 1993 Giovagnoli, 2001; Tsuchiya, Oli, Yahara, Fujieda, 2005; Ilonen, Leinonen, Wallenius, Karlsson, Taiminen, Salokangas, Lauerma, *et al.* 2000) The stimulus cards are always presented from the participant's perspective in a standard left-to-right order: the 1 red triangle, the 2 green stars, the 3 yellow crosses, and the 4 blue circles. The participant is then given a stack of response cards and asked to match each response card to 1 of the stimulus cards. The participant is not told how to match the cards (by the rule of color, form, or number); however, he or she is told whether a particular match is right or wrong.

Administration of the WCST

Research to date supports the use of the WCST in a variety of situations with both children and adults. As an individually administered procedure, the WCST may be used as a clinical or research instrument in combination with other test procedures to assess aspects of cognitive and neuropsychological functioning.

Administration should take place in a quiet room with illumination adequate for viewing the WCST stimuli. Seat the client at the table so that he or she is across from and facing the examiner. Place the stimulus cards on the table in a row in front of the subject. The stimulus cards are always presented from the subject's perspective in a standard left to right order, beginning with the red triangle (on the subject's left), followed by the two green stars, the three yellow crosses, and the four blue circles. The peak of the triangle toward the examiner, the top of the stars point toward the examiner, and the horizontally arranged crosses are closest to the examiner.

After that, the examiner should give the instruction properly, that is; "This is little unusual because I am not allowed to tell you very much about how to do it. You will asked to match each of cards in this deck to one of these key cards. You must take the top card from the deck and place it below the key card you think matches. I cannot tell you how to match the cards, but I will tell you each time whether you are right or wrong. If you are wrong, simply leave the card where you placed it and try to get the next card correct. There is no time limit on this test." Are you ready? Let's begin".

The first correct sorting category is color. As the subject begins to sort the response cards, the examiner responds with "correct" or the "right" each time the client matches to a stimulus dimension other than color. This process continues until the subject has produced 10 consecutive color responses. Without comment or any other indication, the examiner then changes the correct sorting category to form. It is important that the examiner make a smooth and undetectable transition, both verbally and nonverbally, between sorting categories. Form remains as the correct sorting category (principle) until the subject has again attained 10 consecutive correct responses. Without warning or cue as to what is happening, the examiner changes the correct sorting category to number. After 10 consecutive correct responses to number, the examiner will switch back to color as the correct sorting category, and then to form, and then to number in the manner just described. The test continues until the subject has successfully completed six categories or until both decks of response cards have been used, whichever occurs first. If the examiner believes that a subject may be match new response cards to the top card on the response card piles rather than to the stimulus cards, he or she should remind the subject of the correct procedure. This may well be the case if the subject begins to make other responses.

The WCST is not timed, and the subject is informed of this in the instructions. While subjects vary in the amount of time they take to complete the test, most do so within 20-30 minutes.

Recording Responses and Scoring

Accurate recording of a subject's responses is critical to the subsequent scoring of the WCST. In a results of the study of Coehlo *et al.*, (2012) shows that the computerized WCST may not be free of cultural and socioeconomic influences and that the validation and standardization of this version is warranted. The record booklet should be out of the subject's line of vision at all times. As the subject responds to each item, the examiner should draw slashes (/) through each dimension that is the same on both the responses and stimulus cards. For example: CFNO, CFNO, CFNO and CFNO respectively. If the response and stimulus card match on one or more dimensions, a slash should be draw through the symbol on the record booklet that corresponds to that dimensions. For example: CFNO, CFNO. Each correct response should mark side of sheet number 1 to 10 and each incorrect response rounded.

Each response a subject makes can be thought of as occurring on three separate dimensions and, thus, is evaluated on each. These dimensions are: correct-incorrect, ambiguous-unambiguous, and perseverative-non perseverative. Scoring of WCST is based on the manual.

Reliability

With the exception of the learning to learn score (r=0.658), high inters corer reliability coefficients ranged from 0.895 to 1.000 for the 11 scores of the WCST.

Validity

Basic to the validity of a tool is to measure the right thing or asking right questions. The concurrent validity refers to the usefulness of a test in closely relating to other measures or scores on another test of known validity. Thus the WCST has the concurrent validity.

LIMITATION OF THE STUDY

The study has certain limitation that need to be taken into account when considering the study and its contributions.

The selection of the sample was only taken from three districts of Kerala. The list of Students with Learning Disabilities served by school authorities is subjected to screening and after screening the number of the sample was reduced to 40. The study only assess in the areas of strategic planning, organized searching, utilizing environmental feedback to shift cognitive sets, directing behavior toward achieving goal and modulating impulsive responding of executive functions.

THE STATISTICAL TECHNIQUES

The statistical techniques applied for the present study are:

1. Descriptive statistics such as; mean, median, mode and standard deviation, skewness, kurtosis, minimum and maximum scores.
2. To test of group mean difference of variables were calculated by student's t-test.
3. The product moment of correlation coefficient has been used to measure the relationship between the variables.

4

Results

"Research is formalized curiosity. It is poking and prying with a purpose".

– Zora Neale Hurston

INTRODUCTION

The scored data were entered into the master sheet. The scored items were checked individually before entry. The scores were further entered to computer and subjected to analysis through SPSS software to ensure appropriateness.

In the analysis, each objectives and hypothesis of the study were taken into consideration and analyzed with the help of statistical techniques like computation of averages, correlations and t-test to attain best result.

Objective 1: To find out the dimensions of temperament among Students with Learning Disabilities.

Table 4.1: Descriptive statistics of the Effortful Control (EC) scores of temperament among students with Learning Disabilities (N=40)

Descriptive Statistics	Effortful Control (EC)
Mean	30.93
Median	27
Mode	24
Standard Deviation	12.75
Skewness	0.95
Kurtosis	0.27
Minimum	14
Maximum	65

Table 4.1 shows the mean, median, mode, standard deviation, skewness, kurtosis, minimum and maximum scores of Effortful Control (EC) of temperamentamong Students with Learning Disabilities. The total number of Students with Learning Disabilities is 40. The mean and standard deviation of the Effortful Control (EC) scores are 30.93 and 12.75 respectively. The skewness is 0.95 and kurtosis is 0.27, which means that the Effortful Control (EC) scores of the Students with Learning Disabilities spread moderately skewed and nearly to mesokurtic. That is, the Students with Learning Disabilities secured low Effortful Control (EC) scores. The minimum score of Effortful Control (EC) among Students with Learning Disabilities are 14 and the maximum is 65.

Table 4.2: Descriptive statistics of the Surgency (S) scores of temperament among students with Learning Disabilities (N=40)

Descriptive Statistics	Surgency (S)
Mean	35
Median	34
Mode	34
Standard Deviation	8.70
Skewness	-0.06
Kurtosis	0.19
Minimum	15
Maximum	54

From the table 4.2 it is understood thatthe mean, median, mode, standard deviation, skewness, kurtosis, minimum and maximum scores of Surgency (S) of temperament among Students with Learning Disabilities. The total number of Students with Learning Disabilities is 40. The mean of the Surgency (S) scores is 35 and standard deviations is 8.70 respectively. The value of median and mode is34 which is less than the mean value. The skewness is -0.06 and kurtosis is 0.19. It reveals that the Surgency (S) scores of the Students with Learning Disabilities fairly symmetrical and nearly to mesokurtic. It shows that the Students with Learning Disabilities secured low Surgency (S) scores. The minimum score of Surgency (S) among Students with Learning Disabilities is 15 and the maximum is 54.

Table 4.3: Descriptive statistics of the Negative Affect (NA) scores of temperament among students with Learning Disabilities (N=40)

Descriptive Statistics	Negative Affect (NA)
Mean	50.35
Median	50
Mode	50
Standard Deviation	13.53
Skewness	-0.37
Kurtosis	0.42
Minimum	17
Maximum	77

Table 4.3 gives that the mean, median, mode, standard deviation, skewness, kurtosis, minimum and maximum scores of Negative Affect (NA) of temperament among Students with Learning Disabilities. The total number of Students with Learning Disabilities is 40. The mean, median and mode of the Negative Affect (NA) scores are 50.35, 50 and 50 respectively. The standard deviation is 13.53. The skewness is -0.37 and kurtosis is 0.42. These values show that the data seems to be symmetrical and it represents that the Students with Learning Disabilities have high Negative Affect (NA) scores. The minimum score of Negative Affect (NA) among Students with Learning Disabilities are 17 and the maximum is 77.

Table 4.4: Descriptive statistics of the Affiliativeness (AF) scores of temperament among students with Learning Disabilities (N=40)

Descriptive Statistics	Affiliativeness (AF)
Mean	33.08
Median	34
Mode	35
Standard Deviation	6.38
Skewness	0.11
Kurtosis	0.33
Minimum	19
Maximum	48

Table 4.4 depicts that the mean, median, mode, standard deviation, skewness, kurtosis, minimum and maximum scores of Affiliativeness (AF) of temperament among Students with Learning Disabilities. The total number of Students with Learning Disabilities is 40. The mean, median and mode of the Affiliativeness (AF) scores are 33.08, 34 and 35 respectively. The standard deviation is 6.38. The skewness is 0.11 and kurtosis is 0.33. The minimum score of Affiliativeness (AF) among Students with Learning Disabilities are 19 and the maximum is 48.

Objective 2: To find out the temperament among Students with Learning Disabilities.

Table 4.5. Descriptive statistics of the total temperament scores among students with Learning Disabilities (N=40)

Descriptive Statistics	Temperament
Mean	149.35
Median	147.50
Mode	133
Standard Deviation	14.54
Skewness	0.29
Kurtosis	-0.43
Minimum	119
Maximum	181

Table 4.5 shows the Mean, Median, Mode, Standard deviation, Skewness, Kurtosis, Minimum and Maximum scores of total temperament scores among Students with Learning Disabilities. The diagrammatic representation of the data is also given below. The total number of Students with Learning Disabilities was 40. The Mean and Standard Deviation of the temperament total scores are 149.45 and 14.54 respectively. The value of median is 147.50 which is less than the mean value. The Skewness is 0.29 and Kurtosis is -0.43. This means that the temperament total score of the Students with Learning Disabilities spread slightly symmetrical and nearly platykurtic. It shows the total temperament scores of the Students with Learning Disabilities is low. The Minimum score of temperament among Students with Learning Disabilities are 119 and the Maximum is 181.

Objective 3: To find out the dimensions of character among Students with Learning Disabilities

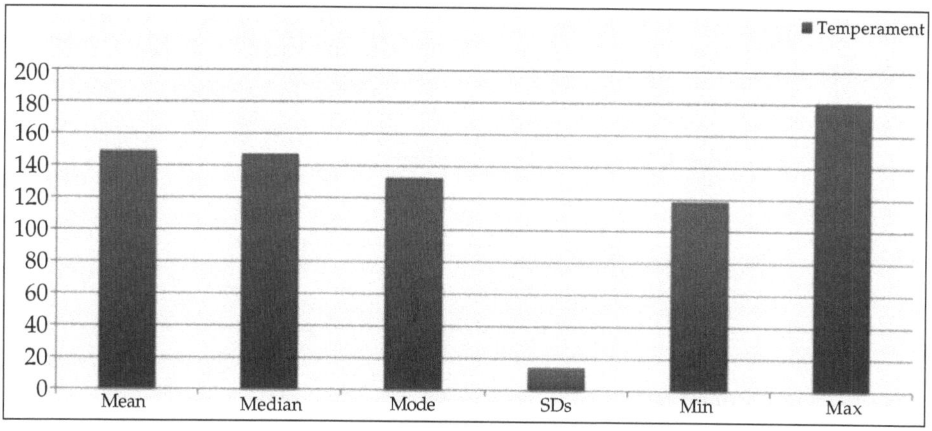

Fig. 4.1: The mean, median, mode, standard deviations, minimum and maximum of total Temperament scores among Students with Learning Disabilities (N=40)

Table 4.6: Descriptive statistics of the Self-Directedness (SD) scores of character among students with Learning Disabilities (N=40)

Descriptive Statistics	Self-Directedness (SD)
Mean	31.65
Median	30.5
Mode	30
Standard Deviation	5.66
Skewness	0.57
Kurtosis	0.09
Minimum	22
Maximum	46

Table 4.6 shows the mean, median, mode, standard deviation, skewness, kurtosis, minimum and maximum scores of Self-Directedness (SD) of characteramong Students with Learning Disabilities. The total number of Students with Learning Disabilities is 40. The mean, median and mode of the Self-Directedness (SD) of character scores is 31.65, 30.5 and 30 respectively. The standard deviation of the Self-Directedness (SD)of character score is 5.66. Mean is higher than the median and mode. Hence the skewness is 0.57 and kurtosis is 0.09. It means that the scores of Self-Directedness (SD) of character among Students with Learning Disabilities are approximately symmetric and they have low scores of Self-Directedness (SD). The minimum score of Self-Directedness (SD)of character scoresamong Students with Learning Disabilities are 22 and the Maximum is 46.

Table 4.7: Descriptive statistics of the Cooperativeness (CO) scores of character among students with Learning Disabilities (N=40)

Descriptive Statistics	Cooperativeness (CO)
Mean	32.33
Median	32.5
Mode	38
Standard Deviation	5.56
Skewness	-0.25
Kurtosis	-0.74
Minimum	21
Maximum	43

From the table 4.7, it is seen that the mean, median, mode, standard deviation, skewness, kurtosis, minimum and maximum scores of Cooperativeness (CO) of characteramong Students with Learning Disabilities. The total number of Students with Learning Disabilities is 40. The mean of the Cooperativeness (CO) of character scores is 32.33 and standard deviation of the Cooperativeness (CO) scores of character is 5.56. The value of median is 32.5, mode is 38 which is higher than the mean value. Hence the skewness is -0.25 and kurtosis is -0.74. The Cooperativeness (CO) of character scores among the Students with Learning Disabilities is negatively skewed and the data falls on platykurtic. That is the Students with Learning Disabilities have low Cooperativeness (CO) of character scores. The minimum score of Cooperativeness (CO) of character scoresamong Students with Learning Disabilities are 21 and the Maximum is 43.

Table 4.8: Descriptive statistics of the Self-Transcendence (ST) scores of character among students with Learning Disabilities (N=40)

Descriptive Statistics	Self-Transcendence (ST)
Mean	16.18
Median	17
Mode	19
Standard Deviation	4.55
Skewness	-0.15
Kurtosis	-0.74
Minimum	7
Maximum	25

Table 4.8 shows the mean, median, mode, standard deviation, skewness, kurtosis, minimum and maximum scores of Self-Transcendence (ST) of character among Students with Learning Disabilities. The total number of Students with Learning Disabilities is 40. The mean, median and mode of the Self-Transcendence (ST) of character scores are 16.18, 17 and 19 respectively. The standard deviation of the Self-Transcendence (ST) of character score is 4.55. Mean is less than the median and mode. Hence the skewness is -0.15. The kurtosis is -0.74. It reveals that the Self-Transcendence (ST) of character scores among Students with Learning Disabilities islow. The minimum score of Self-Transcendence (ST) of character scores among Students with Learning Disabilities is7 and the Maximum is 25.

Objective 4: To find out the characteramong Students with Learning Disabilities

Table 4.9: Descriptive statistics of the total character scores among students with Learning Disabilities (N=40)

Descriptive Statistics	Character
Mean	80.15
Median	78
Mode	74
Standard Deviation	12.96
Skewness	0.29
Kurtosis	-0.67
Minimum	59
Maximum	106

From the table 4.9 shows the mean, median, mode, standard deviation, skewness, kurtosis, minimum and maximum scores of character total scores among Students with Learning Disabilities. The total number of Students with Learning Disabilities was 40. The mean of the character total score is 80.15 and standard deviation of the character total score is 12.96. The value of median is 78 which is less than the mean value. The skewness is 0.29 and Kurtosis is -0.67. It is very clear that the total character score of the Students with Learning Disabilities is slightly symmetrical and platykurtic. It clear shows that the character total score is low. The Minimum score of character among Students with Learning Disabilities are 59 and the Maximum is 106. A figure is given below from the above details.

Objective 5: To find out the dimensions of temperament among Students without Learning Disabilities.

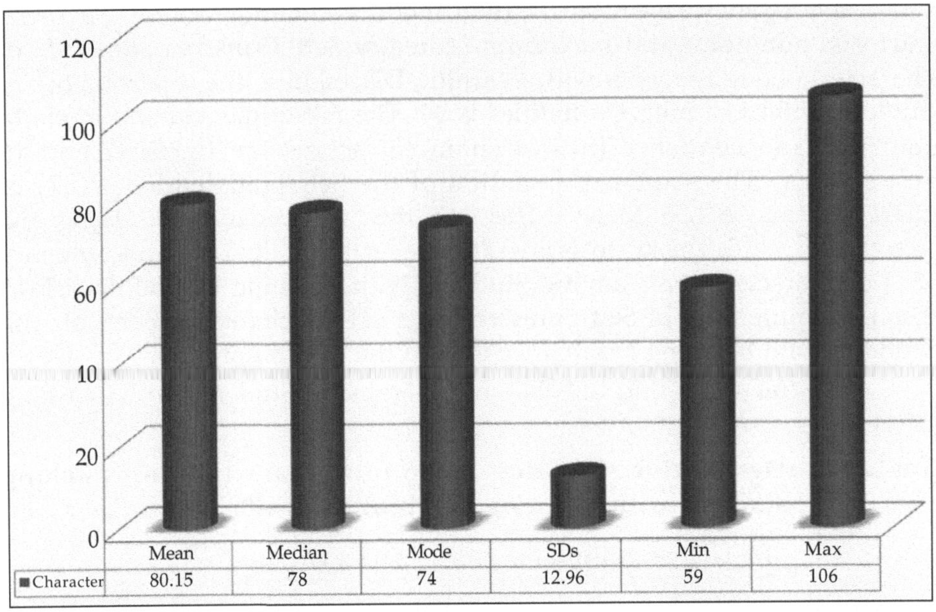

Fig. 4.2: The mean, median, mode, standard deviations, minimum and maximum of total Character scores among Students with Learning Disabilities (N=40)

Table 4.10: Descriptive Statistics regarding the Effortful Control (EC) scores of temperament among students without Learning Disabilities (N=40)

Descriptive Statistics	Effortful Control (EC)
Mean	52.43
Median	54.50
Mode	55
Standard Deviation	8.07
Skewness	-0.82
Kurtosis	0.39
Minimum	30
Maximum	67

From the above table 4.10 gives the information of the mean, median, mode, standard deviation, skewness, kurtosis, minimum and maximum scores of Effortful Control (EC) of temperament among Students without Learning Disabilities. The total number of Students without Learning Disabilities is 40. The mean and standard deviation of the Effortful Control (EC) of temperament score is 52.43 and 8.07 respectively. The value of median is 54.50 and the mode is 55. The skewness is -0.82 and kurtosis is 0.39. It means that the Effortful Control (EC) of temperament among Students without Learning Disabilities is high. The minimum score of Effortful Control (EC) of temperament dimensions among Students without Learning Disabilities is 30 and the Maximum is 67.

Table 4.11: Descriptive Statistics regarding the Surgency (S) scores of temperament among students without Learning Disabilities (N=40)

Descriptive Statistics	Surgency (S)
Mean	39.13
Median	38
Mode	34
Standard Deviation	6.20
Skewness	0.19
Kurtosis	-1.11
Minimum	29
Maximum	50

Table 4.11 gives the mean, median, mode, standard deviation, skewness, kurtosis, minimum and maximum scores of Surgency (S) of temperament among Students without Learning Disabilities. The total number of Students without Learning Disabilities is 40.The mean of the Surgency (S) scores is 39.13 and standard deviations is 6.20 respectively. The value of median is 38 and mode is 34 which is less than the mean value. The skewness is 0.19 and kurtosis is -1.11. It means that the Surgency (S) scores of the Students without Learning Disabilities moderately skewed and it is leptokurtic. That is, they have high Surgency (S) of temperament. The minimum score of Surgency (S) among Students without Learning Disabilities are 29 and the maximum is 50.

Table 4.12: Descriptive Statistics regarding the Negative Affect (NA) scores of Temperament among students without Learning Disabilities (N=40)

Descriptive Statistics	Negative Affect (NA)
Mean	46.10
Median	46.50
Mode	40
Standard Deviation	10.39
Skewness	-0.31
Kurtosis	-0.50
Minimum	22
Maximum	64

It is seen that the table 4.12 shows the mean, median, mode, standard deviation, skewness, kurtosis, minimum and maximum scores of Negative Affect (NA) of temperament among Students without Learning Disabilities. The total number of Students without Learning Disabilities is 40. The mean, median and mode of the Negative Affect (NA) scores is 46.10, 46.50 and 40 respectively. The standard deviations are 10.39. The skewness is -0.31 and kurtosis is -0.50. It means that the Negative Affect (NA) of temperament among Students without Learning Disabilities is low. The minimum score of Negative Affect (NA) among Students without Learning Disabilities are 22 and the maximum is 64.

Table 4.13: Descriptive statistics of the Affiliativeness (AF) scores of temperament among students without Learning Disabilities (N=40)

Descriptive Statistics	Affiliativeness (AF)
Mean	34.48
Median	34.50
Mode	27
Standard Deviation	6.34
Skewness	-0.21
Kurtosis	-0.56
Minimum	21
Maximum	46

Table 4.13 reveals the mean, median, mode, standard deviation, skewness, kurtosis, minimum and maximum scores of Affiliativeness (AF) of temperament among Students without Learning Disabilities. The total number of Students without Learning Disabilities is 40.The mean, median and mode of the Affiliativeness (AF) scores are 34.48, 34.50 and 27 respectively. The standard deviations are 6.34. The skewness is -0.21 and kurtosis is -0.56. The minimum score of Affiliativeness (AF) among Students without Learning Disabilities are 21 and the maximum is 46.

Objective 6: To find out the temperament among Students without Learning Disabilities.

Table 4.14 shows the Mean, Median, Mode, Standard deviation, Skewness, Kurtosis, Minimum and Maximum scores of temperament among Students without Learning Disabilities. The total number of Students without Learning Disabilities is 40. The Mean and Standard Deviation of the temperament total score is 172.12 and 13.48 respectively. The value of median is 172.50. The Skewness is -0.51 and kurtosis is 0.53. It depicts that the temperament total score of the Students without Learning Disabilities spread fairly symmetrical and also its leptokurtic. That is the temperament total score of the Students without Learning Disabilities is high. The minimum total score of temperament among Students without Learning Disabilities is 134 and the Maximum is 197. The above data are shown in the figure 4.3.

Table 4.14: Descriptive statistics regarding the total temperament scores among students without Learning Disabilities (N=40)

Descriptive Statistics	Temperament
Mean	172.12
Median	172.50
Mode	172
Standard Deviation	13.48
Skewness	-0.51
Kurtosis	0.53
Minimum	134
Maximum	197

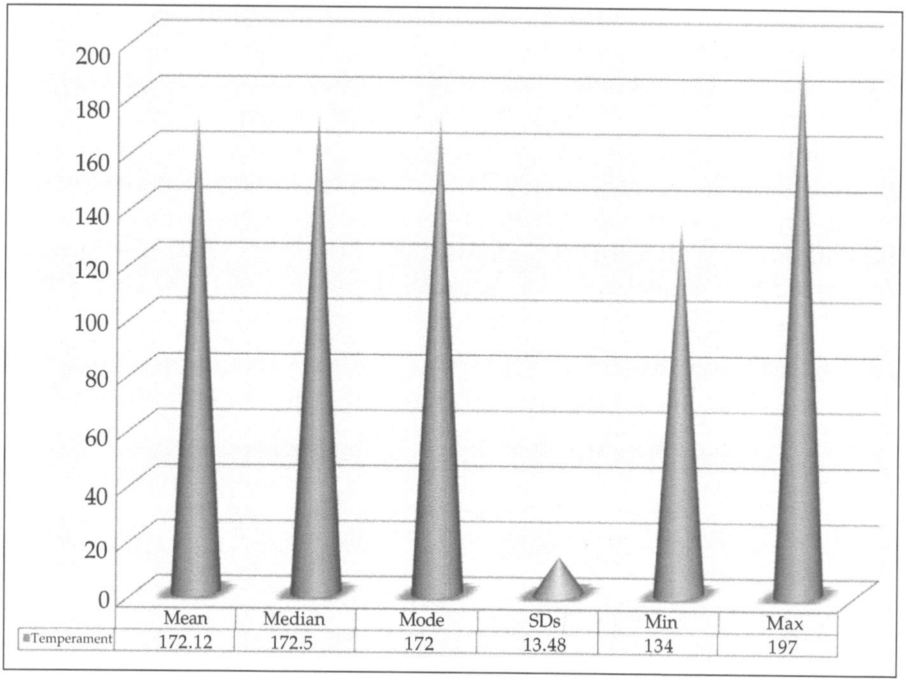

Fig. 4.3: The mean, median, mode, standard deviations, minimum and maximum of total Temeperament scores among Students without Learning Disabilities (N=40)

Objective 7: To find out the dimensions of character among Students without Learning Disabilities

Table 4.15: Descriptive statistics of the Self-Directedness (SD) scores of character among students without Learning Disabilities (N=40)

Descriptive Statistics	Self-Directedness (SD)
Mean	39.68
Median	40
Mode	40
Standard Deviation	5.71
Skewness	-0.84
Kurtosis	1.38
Minimum	21
Maximum	48

From the table 4.15 describes the mean, median, mode, standard deviation, skewness, kurtosis, minimum and maximum scores of Self-Directedness (SD) score of character among Students without Learning Disabilities. The total number of Students without Learning Disabilities is 40. The meanof the Self-Directedness (SD) of character scores is 39.68. The median and mode of the Self-Directedness (SD) of character scores are 40. The standard deviation of the Self-Directedness (SD) of character score is 5.71. The skewness is -0.84 whereas kurtosis is 1.38. That is, the Students without Learning Disabilities have high Self-Directedness (SD) of character score. The minimum score of Self-Directedness (SD) of character dimension scores among Students without Learning Disabilities are 21 and the Maximum is 48.

Table 4.16: Descriptive statistics of the Cooperativeness (CO) scores of character among students without Learning Disabilities (N=40)

Descriptive Statistics	Cooperativeness (CO)
Mean	40.75
Median	41.5
Mode	37
Standard Deviation	6.82
Skewness	-0.52
Kurtosis	0.79
Minimum	21
Maximum	54

Table 4.16 gives that the mean, median, mode, standard deviation, skewness, kurtosis, minimum and maximum scores of Cooperativeness (CO) scores of character among Students without Learning Disabilities. The total number of Students without Learning Disabilities is 40.The mean of the Cooperativeness (CO) of character scores is 40.75 and standard deviation of the Cooperativeness (CO) of character score is 6.82. The value of median is 41.5 mode is 37 which is higher than the mean value. Hence the skewness is -0.52, therefore the data negatively skewed. The kurtosis is 0.79. The details reveals that the Cooperativeness (CO) scores of character among Students without Learning Disabilities is high. The minimum score of Cooperativeness (CO) of character scores among Students without Learning Disabilities are 21 and the maximum is 54.

Table 4.17: Descriptive statistics of the Self-Transcendence (ST) scores of character among students without Learning Disabilities (N=40)

Descriptive Statistics	Self-Transcendence (ST)
Mean	19.43
Median	19.50
Mode	17
Standard Deviation	3.95
Skewness	0.15
Kurtosis	1.34
Minimum	9
Maximum	31

Table 4.17 shows the mean, median, mode, standard deviation, skewness, kurtosis, minimum and maximum scores of Self-Transcendence (ST) scores of character among Students without Learning Disabilities. The total number of Students without Learning Disabilities is 40. The mean, median and mode of the Self-Transcendence (ST) of character scores are 19.43, 19.50, and 17 respectively. The standard deviation of the Self-Transcendence (ST) of character score is 3.95. The skewness is 0.15 and the kurtosis is 1.34. That is the Self-Transcendence (ST) scores of character among Students without Learning Disabilities are high. The minimum and maximum score of Self-Transcendence (ST) of character dimension among Students without Learning Disabilities are 9 and 31 respectively.

Objective 8: To find out the character among Students without Learning Disabilities.

Table 4.20: Descriptive statistics of the total number of error responses of executive functions among students with Learning Disabilities (N=40)

Descriptive Statistics	Total Number of Error Response
Mean	53.20
Median	54
Mode	66
Standard Deviation	17.47
Skewness	-0.44
Kurtosis	-0.29
Minimum	17
Maximum	84

Table 4.20 shows the Mean, Median, Mode, Standard deviation, Skewness, Kurtosis, Minimum and Maximum scores of total number of error response of executive functions among Students with Learning Disabilities. The Mean of the total number of error responses are 53.20. The median of the total number of error responses is 54. The value of Mode is 66 and Standard Deviation and is 17.47. Skewness is -0.44, whereas kurtosis is -0.29, that is they have above average level of error responses of executive functions. The minimum score of number of error response are 44 and the maximum is 110. The described details are shown in the figure 4.6.

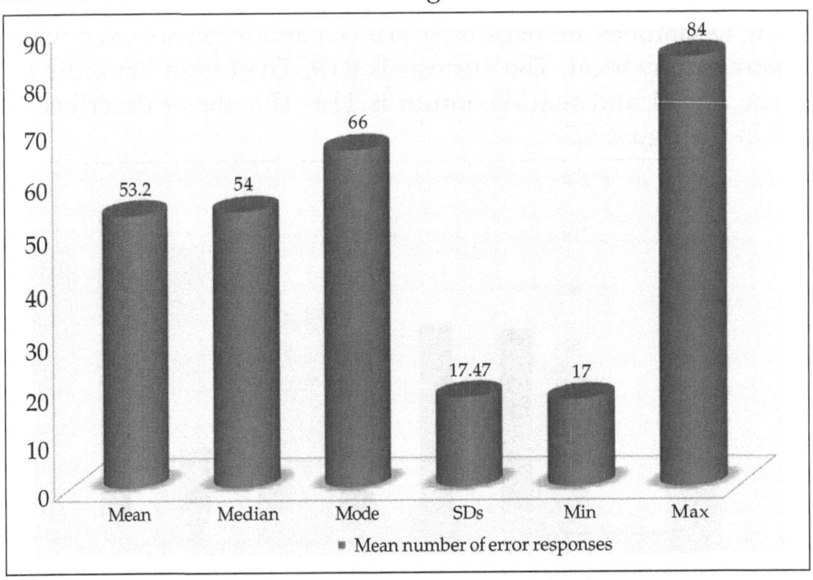

Fig. 4.6: The descriptive statistics of the total number of error responses of Executive Functions among students with Learning Disabilities (N=40)

Table 4.21: Descriptive statistics of the perseverative responses of executive functions among students with Learning Disabilities (N=40)

Descriptive Statistics	Perseverative Responses
Mean	31.95
Median	32
Mode	28
Standard Deviation(SD)	11.60
Skewness	0.29
Kurtosis	0.86
Minimum	9
Maximum	66

Table 4.21 shows the Mean, Median, Mode, Standard deviation, Skewness, Kurtosis, Minimum and Maximum scores of perseverative responses of executive functions among Students with Learning Disabilities. The Mean of the perseverative responses are 31.25. The median of the perseverative responses of executive functions are 32. The value of Mode is 28 and Standard Deviation and is 11.60. The skewness is 0.29 and Kurtosis is 0.86. That is the peseverative responses of executive functions among Students with Learning Disabilities is above average level. The minimum score of peseverative responses is 9 and the maximum is 66.

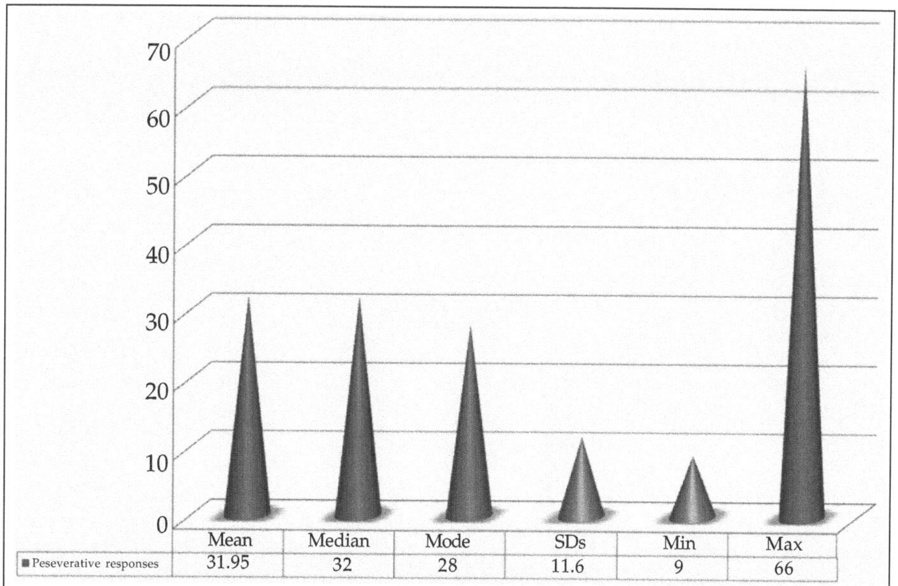

Fig. 4.7: The mean, median, mode, SDs, minimum and maximum of the perseverative responses of Executive Functions among Students with Learning Disabilities (N=40)

Table 4.22: Descriptive statistics of the perseverative error responses of executive functions among students with Learning Disabilities (N=40)

Descriptive Statistics	Perseverative Error Response
Mean	28.27
Median	30
Mode	31
Standard Deviation	9.90
Skewness	0.35
Kurtosis	1.33
Minimum	8
Maximum	59

Table 4.22 shows the Mean, Median, Mode, Standard deviation, Skewness, Kurtosis, Minimum and Maximum scores of peseverative error responses of executive functions among Students with Learning Disabilities. The Mean of the peseverative error responses is 28.27. The median of the peseverative error responses of executive functions is 30. The value of Mode is 31 and Standard Deviation is 9.90. Skewness is 0.35and the kurtosis is 1.33. Hence the perseverative error responses of executive functions among Students with Learning Disabilities is above average level and the minimum score of peseverative error responses is 8 and the maximum is 59, which is presented in the figure 4.8.

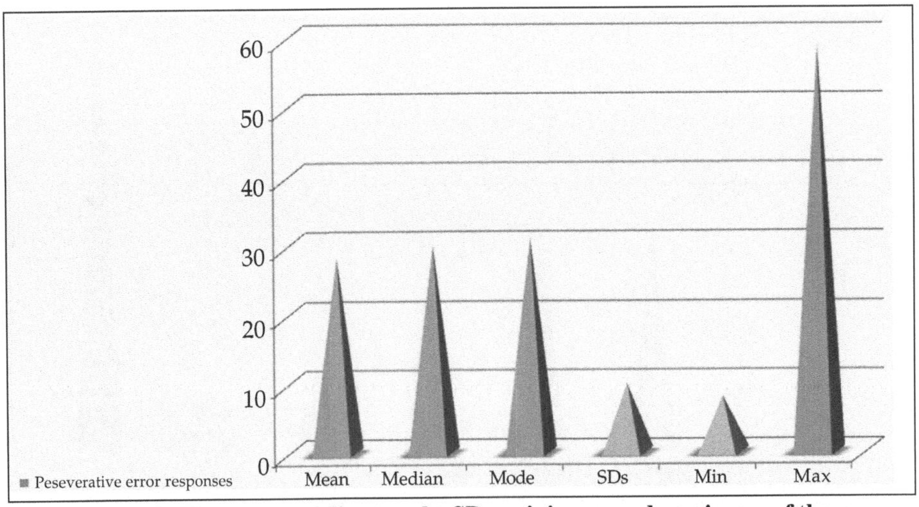

Fig. 4.8: The mean, median, mode, SDs, minimum and maximum of the Perseverative error responses of Executive Functions among students with Learning Disabilities (N=40)

Table 4.23: Descriptive statistics of the non perseverative response of executive functions among students with Learning Disabilities (N=40)

Descriptive statistics	Non Perseverative Response
Mean	24.7
Median	22
Mode	12
Standard Deviation	14.54
Skewness	0.87
Kurtosis	0.47
Minimum	5
Maximum	65

Table 4.23 shows the Mean, Median, Mode, Standard deviation, Skewness, Kurtosis, Minimum and Maximum scores of non-perseverative response of executive functions among Students with Learning Disabilities. The Mean of the non-perseverative response is 24.7. The median of the non perseverative response of executive functions is 22. The value of Mode is 12 and Standard Deviation and is 14.54. Skewness is 0.87. The kurtosis is 0.47. It reveals that the non-perseverative response of executive functions among Students with Learning Disabilities is above average level. The minimum score non perseverative response is 5 and the maximum is 65. The figure is given below.

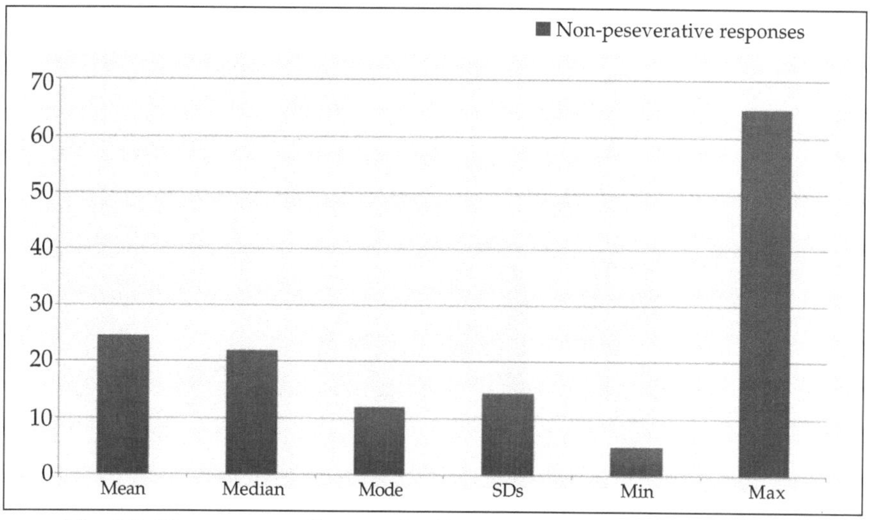

Fig. 4.9: The mean, median, mode, SDs, minimum and maximum of the Non perseverative responseof Executive Functions among Students with Learning Disabilities (N=40)

Table 4.24: Descriptive statistics of the conceptual level response of executive functions among students with Learning Disabilities (N=40)

Descriptive Statistics	Conceptual Level Response
Mean	35.6
Median	31
Mode	31
Standard Deviation	15.68
Skewness	0.88
Kurtosis	0.59
Minimum	11
Maximum	82

Table 4.24 shows the Mean, Median, Mode, Standard deviation, Skewness, Kurtosis, Minimum and Maximum scores of conceptual level response of executive functions among Students with Learning Disabilities. The Mean of the conceptual level response is 35.6. The median of the conceptual level response of executive functions is 31. The value of Mode is 31 and Standard Deviation and is 15.68. Skewness is 0.88 and the kurtosis is 0.59. It means that the scores of conceptual level among Students with Learning Disabilities is below average level. The minimum score conceptual level response is 11 and the maximum is 82.

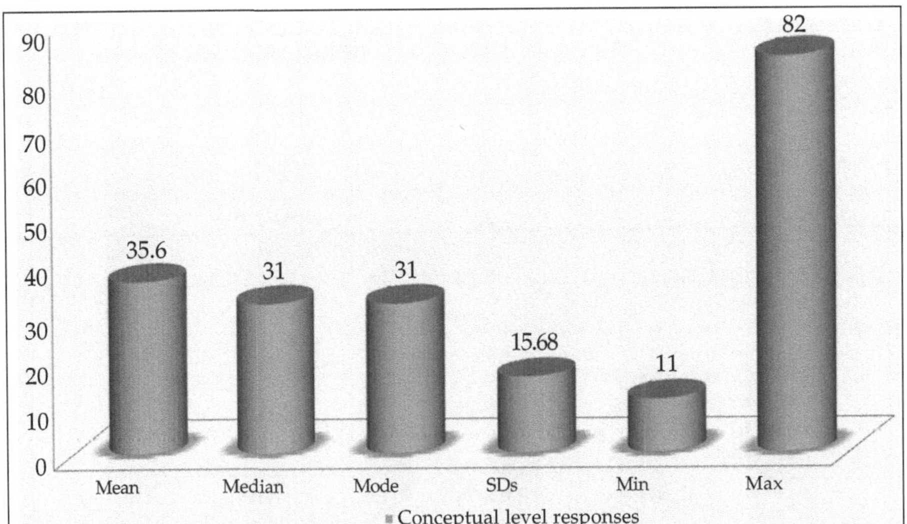

Fig. 4.10: The mean, median, mode, SDs, minimum and maximum of the Conceptual level responseof Executive Functions among Students with Learning Disabilities (N=40)

Objective 10: To find out certain selected executive functions among Students without Learning Disabilities.

Table 4.25: Descriptive statistics of the total number of correct responses of Executive functions among students without Learning Disabilities (N=40)

Descriptive Statistics	Total Number of Correct Responses
Mean	92.70
Median	93.50
Mode	79
Standard Deviation	12.98
Skewness	-0.72
Kurtosis	0.58
Minimum	54
Maximum	113

Table 4.25 shows the Mean, Median, Mode, Standard deviation, Skewness, Kurtosis, Minimum and Maximum scores of total number of correct response of executive functions among Students without Learning Disabilities. The Mean and Standard Deviation of the correct responses are 92.70 and 12.98 respectively. It clearly shows that the total number of correct response of executive functions among Students without Learning Disabilities is above average level. The value of median is 93.50, which is higher to the mean value. The value of Mode is 79, Skewness is -0.72. The kurtosis is 0.58. It shows that the scores of total number of correct response of executive functions among Students without Learning Disabilities is above average level. The minimum score of correct response are 54 and the maximum is 113. These details are given in the figure 4.11.

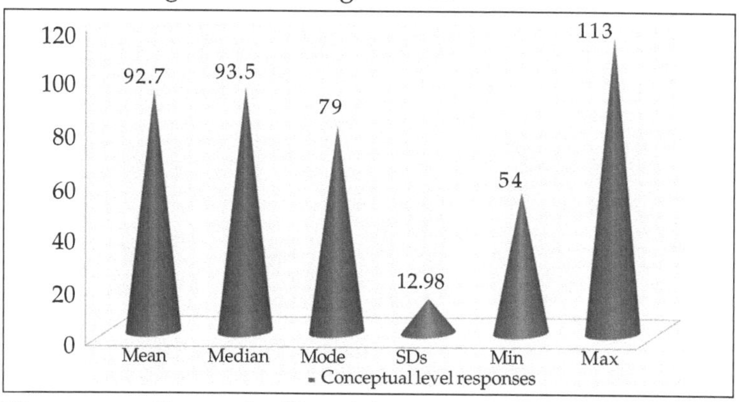

Fig. 4.11: The mean, median, mode, SDs, minimum and maximum of the Total Number of correct responses of Executive Functions among Students without Learning Disabilities (N=40)

Table 4.26: Descriptive statistics of the total number of error responses of executive functions among students without Learning Disabilities (N=40)

Descriptive Statistics	Total Number of Error Response
Mean	34.80
Median	33.50
Mode	23
Standard Deviation	13.12
Skewness	0.78
Kurtosis	0.59
Minimum	15
Maximum	74

Table 4.26 shows the Mean, Median, Mode, Standard deviation, Skewness, Kurtosis, Minimum and Maximum scores of total number of error response of executive functions among Students without Learning Disabilities. The mean of the total number of error responses is 34.50. The median of the total number of error responses is 33.50. The value of mode is 23 and standard deviation is 13.12. It shows that the total number of error response of executive functions among Students without Learning Disabilities is below average level. Skewness and kurtosis are 0.78, 0.59 respectively. The minimum score of number of error response are 15and the maximum is 74.

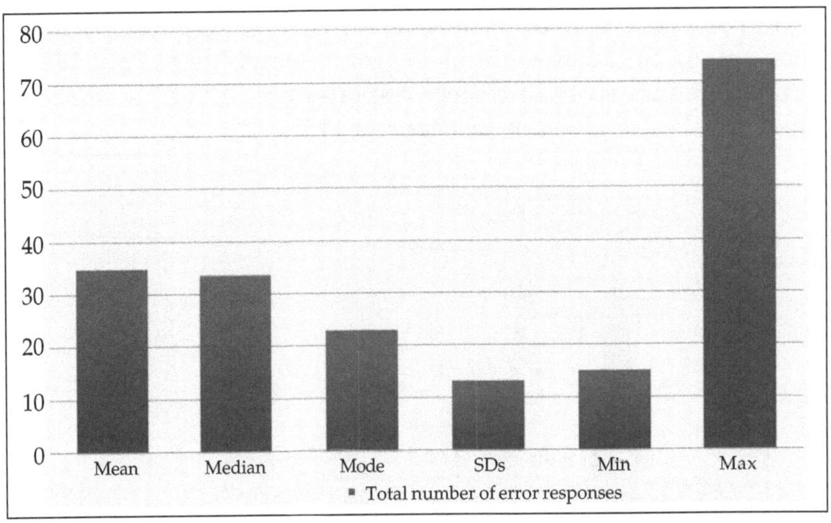

Fig. 4.12: The mean, median, mode, SDs, minimum and maximum of the Total Number of error responses of Executive Functions among Students without Learning Disabilities (N=40)

Table 4.27: Descriptive statistics of the Peseverative responses of Executive Functions among Students without Learning Disabilities (N=40)

Descriptive Statistics	Perseverative Responses
Mean	18.40
Median	17.50
Mode	17
Standard Deviation	6.31
Skewness	0.27
Kurtosis	-0.65
Minimum	7
Maximum	30

Table 4.27 shows the Mean, Median, Mode, Standard deviation, Skewness, Kurtosis, Minimum and Maximum scores of perseverative responses of executive functions among Students without Learning Disabilities. The mean of the perseverative responses is 18.40. The median of the perseverative responses of executive functions is 17.50. The value of Mode is 17 and Standard Deviation is 6.31. Skewness is 0.27and Kurtosis is -0.65. It reveals that the perseverative responses of executive functions among Students without Learning Disabilities are below average level. The minimum score of perseverative responsesis 7 and the maximum is 30.

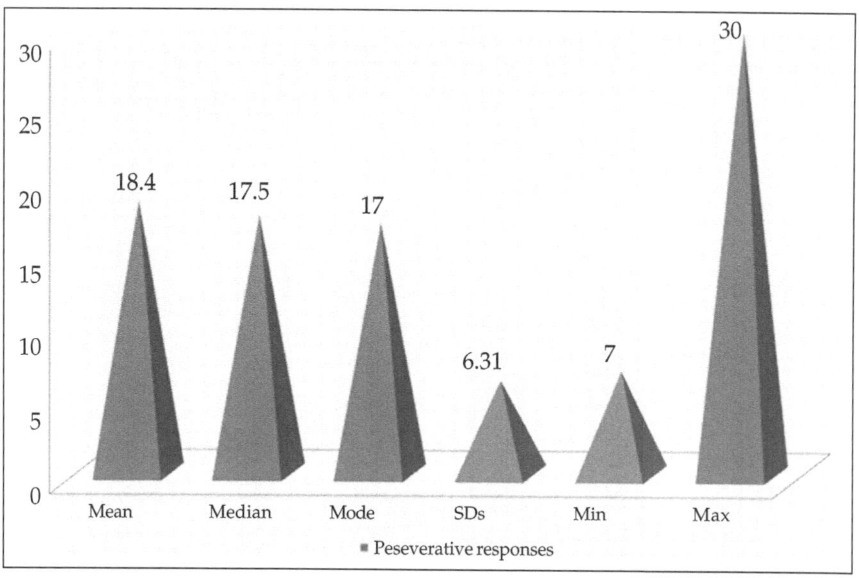

Fig. 4.13: The mean, median, mode, SDs, minimum and maximum of the Peseverative responses of Executive Functions among Students without Learning Disabilities (N=40)

Table 4.28: Descriptive statistics of the perseverative error responses of executive functions among students without Learning Disabilities (N=40)

Descriptive Statistics	Perseverative Error Response
Mean	15.40
Median	14.50
Mode	13
Standard Deviation	6.05
Skewness	0.63
Kurtosis	0.05
Minimum	5
Maximum	28

Table 4.28 shows the Mean, Median, Mode, Standard deviation, Skewness, Kurtosis, Minimum and Maximum scores of perseverative error responses of executive functions among Students without Learning Disabilities. The mean of the perseverative error responses is 15.40. The median of the perseverative error responses of executive functions is 14.50. The value of mode is 13 and Standard Deviation is 6.05. Skewness is 0.63 and kurtosis is 0.05. It clearly shows that the perseverative error responses of executive functions among Students without Learning Disabilities are below average level. The minimum score of perseverative error responsesis 5 and the Maximum is 28. The above details are give in the figure 4.14.

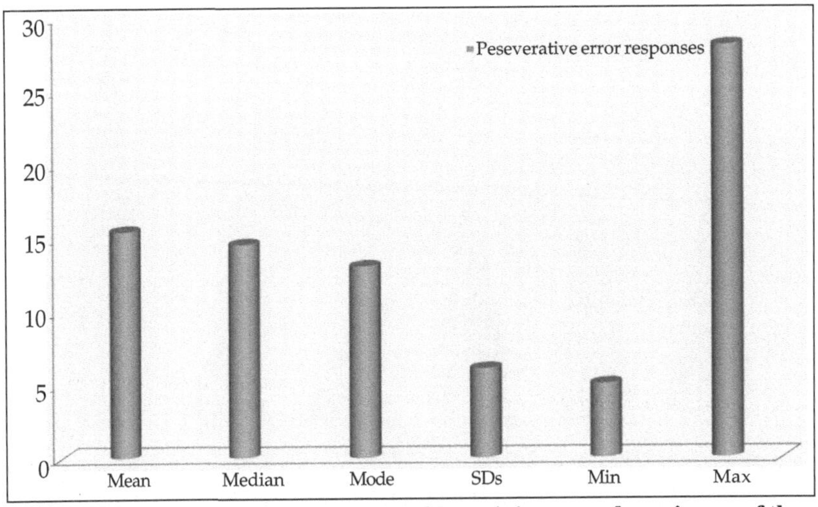

Fig. 4.14: The mean, median, mode, SDs, minimum and maximum of the Perseverative error responses of Executive Functions among Students without Learning Disabilities (N=40)

Table 4.29: Descriptive statistics of the Non perseverative response of executive functions among students without Learning Disabilities (N=40)

Descriptive Statistics	Non Perseverative Response
Mean	19.25
Median	15.50
Mode	9
Standard Deviation	10.27
Skewness	0.75
Kurtosis	0.02
Minimum	5
Maximum	48

Table 4.29 shows the Mean, Median, Mode, Standard deviation, Skewness, Kurtosis, Minimum and Maximum scores of non perseverative response of executive functions among Students without Learning Disabilities. The Mean of the non perseverative response is 19.25. The median of the non perseverative response of executive functions is 15.50. The value of Mode is 9 and Standard Deviation is 10.27. Skewness is 0.75 and kurtosis is 0.02, which shows that the non perseverative response of executive functions among Students without Learning Disabilities is below average level. The minimum score non perseverative response is 5 and the maximum is 48. The above described data are graphically represented in the figure 4.15.

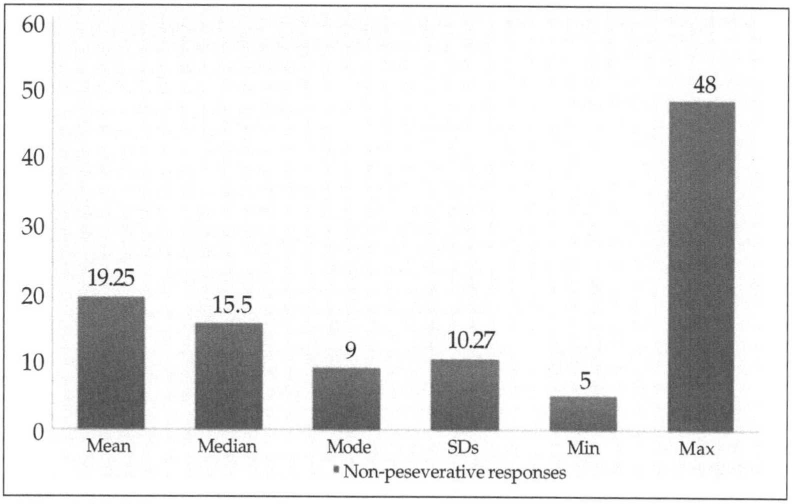

Fig. 4.15: The mean, median, mode, SDs, minimum and maximum of the Non perseverative responses of Executive Functions among Students without Learning Disabilities (N=40)

Table 4.30: Descriptive statistics of the conceptual level response of executive functions among students without Learning Disabilities (N=40)

Descriptive Statistics	Conceptual Level Response
Mean	69.78
Median	70.50
Mode	92
Standard Deviation	18.03
Skewness	-0.04
Kurtosis	-1.52
Minimum	38
Maximum	97

Table 4.30 shows the Mean, Median, Mode, Standard deviation, Skewness, Kurtosis, Minimum and Maximum scores of conceptual level response of executive functions among Students with Learning Disabilities. The Mean of the conceptual level response is 69.78. The median of the conceptual level response of executive functions are 70.50. The value of Mode is 92 and Standard Deviation is 18.03. Skewness is -0.04. The kurtosis is - 1.52, it means that the conceptual level response of executive functions among Students with Learning Disabilities is above average level. The minimum score conceptual level response is 38 and the maximum is 97.

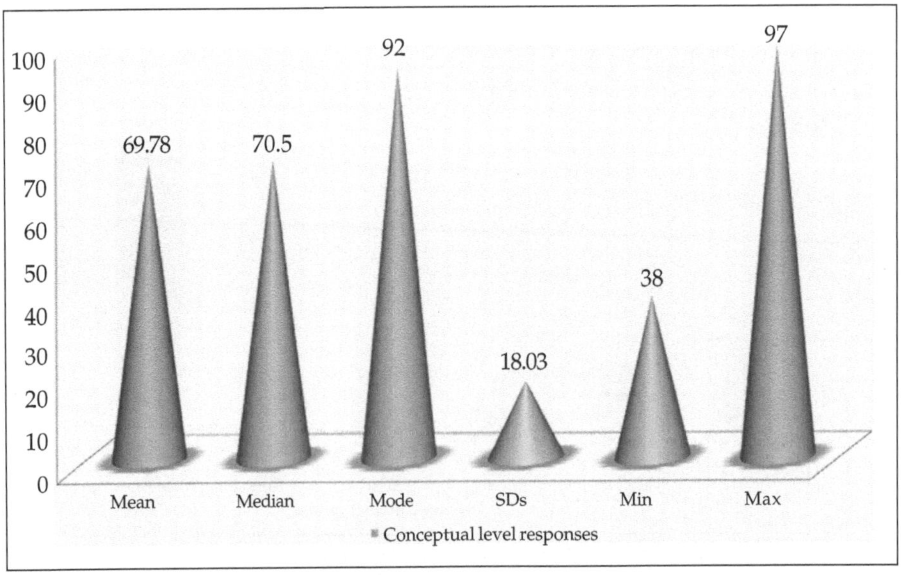

Fig. 4.16: The mean, median, mode, SDs, minimum and maximum of theConceptual level responses of Executive Functions among Students without Learning Disabilities (N=40)

Objective 11: To find out the relation between dimensions of temperament and certain selected executive functions among Students with Learning Disabilities.

H0 1: There will be no relation between the dimensions of temperament and certain selected executive functions among Students with Learning Disabilities.

Table 4.31: Correlation coefficient of the Effortful Control (EC) of temperament and executive functions among students with Learning Disabilities (N=40)

Executive Functions	Effortful Control (EC)
Total number of correct responses	0.49**
Total number of error responses	-0.31
Perseverative responses	-0.11
Perseverative error response	-0.13
Non perseverative response	-0.28
Conceptual level response	0.58**

**. Correlation is significant at the 0.01 level.

Table 4.31 shows that the correlation coefficient of the Effortful Control (EC) of temperament and executive functions among Students with Learning Disabilities. The correlation coefficient of total number of correct responses of executive functions and Effortful Control (EC) of temperament is 0.49, which is significant at 0.01 levels. Hence the null hypothesis is rejected. That means there is a positive relationship between Effortful Control (EC) of temperament and the total number of correct response of executive functions. That is the students who have high in any areas of the Effortful Control (EC) of temperament like; attention, inhibitory control and activation control make more correct response. The correlation coefficient of total number of error responses of executive functions and Effortful Control (EC) of temperament is -0.31, which is not significant at any levels. The correlation coefficient of perseverative responses of executive functions and Effortful Control (EC) of temperament is -0.11, which is also not significant at any levels. The correlation coefficient of perseverative error responses of executive functions and Effortful Control (EC) of temperament is -0.13, which is not significant. The correlation coefficient of non perseverative response is -0.28. That is, there is no significant relationship between the temperament and non perseverative response of executive function. But in the case of conceptual level of response, the correlation coefficient of conceptual level of response of students with learning disabilities is 0.58, which is significant at 0.01 levels. There is a positive relationship between Effortful Control (EC) of temperament and conceptual level response of executive functions among students with learning disabilities. The above detail clearly shows that there is a moderate relationship between Effortful Control (EC) of temperament and executive functions among Students with Learning Disabilities. Studies are shown that Effortful Control (EC) and inhibitory control of temperament over behaviours, cognitions and emotions is related to the attentional process of focus and flexibly switch attention. These attentional processes play a supportive role in adjustment and learning. That is, shift attention from immediately rewarding stimuli to focus on the task (Rothbart & Ahadi, 1994, Rothbart *et al.*, 2001).

Table 4.32: Correlation coefficient of the Surgency (S) of temperament and executive functions among students with Learning Disabilities (N=40)

Executive Functions	Surgency (S)
Total number of correct responses	-0.09
Total number of error responses	-0.15
Perseverative responses	-0.35*
Perseverative error response	-0.35*
Non perseverative response	0.06
Conceptual level response	-0.08

*. Correlation is significant at the 0.05 level.

Table 4.32 shows that the correlation coefficient of the Surgency (S) of temperament and executive functions among Students with Learning Disabilities. The correlation coefficients of total number of correct responses, error responses, non perseverative response and conceptual level responses with Surgency (S) of temperament are -0.09, -0.15, 0.06 and -0.08 respectively. From the table which is clear that the correlation coefficient of perseverative responses and perseverative error responsesof executive functions and Surgency (S) of temperament is -0.35 and these are only significant at 0.05 levels. Hence the null hypothesis is rejected. Both shows the significant negative correlations. Some studies shows the same results related to academic difficulties. That is high levels of activity have been related with increased risk for externalizing behavioural problems and may predispose individuals to interpersonal and academic difficulties (Moss, Blackston, Martin & Tarter, 1992; Tarter, 1988).

Table 4.33: Correlation coefficient of the Negative Affect (NA) of temperament and executive functions among students with Learning Disabilities (N=40)

Executive Functions	Negative Affect (NA)
Total number of correct responses	-0.09
Total number of error responses	0.12
Perseverative responses	0.11
Perseverative error response	0.10
Non perseverative response	0.06
Conceptual level response	-0.29

Table 4.33 shows that the correlation coefficient of the Negative Affect (NA) of temperament and executive functions among Students with Learning Disabilities. From the table which is clear that there is a no significant correlation between the Negative Affect (NA) of temperament and executive functions among Students with Learning Disabilities. The values only shows that the weak correlations. The correlation coefficient of total number of correct responses and Negative Affect (NA) of temperament is -0.09. The correlation coefficient of total number of error responses and Negative Affect (NA) of temperament is 0.12. The coefficient of perseverative responses and Negative Affect (NA) of temperament is 0.11 and perseverative error responses of executive functions and Negative Affect (NA) of temperament is 0.10.In the case of non perseverative response, and conceptual level responses with Negative Affect (NA) of temperament are 0.06 and -0.29 respectively. Hence the null hypothesis is accepted.

Table 4.34: Correlation coefficient of the Affiliativeness (AF) of temperament and executive functions among students with Learning Disabilities (N=40)

Executive Functions	Affiliativeness (AF)
Total number of correct responses	0.29
Total number of error responses	-0.32*
Perseverative responses	-0.28
Perseverative error response	-0.22
Non perseverative response	-0.22
Conceptual level response	0.44**

**. Correlation is significant at the 0.01 level.

*. Correlation is significant at the 0.05 level.

Table 4.34 shows that the correlation coefficient of the Affiliativeness (AF) of temperament and executive functions among Students with Learning Disabilities. From the table which is clear that the correlation coefficient of total number of error response and Affiliativeness (AF) of temperament is -0.32 which is significant at 0.05 level. Hence the null hypothesis is rejected. It indicates that the significant negative correlation. That means, those who have low Affiliativeness (AF) of temperament leads make more error response of executive functions. That is the Students with Learning Disabilities, those who have in low affiliation, perceptual sensitivity and pleasure sensitivity of Affiliativeness (AF) dimension of temperament make more errors of executive functions. The correlation coefficient of conceptual level response and Affiliativeness (AF)of temperament is 0.44 which is significant at 0.01 levels. That means there exists a significant positive correlation. This indicates that the Students with Learning Disabilities who have in high score in affiliation, perceptual sensitivity and pleasure sensitivity of Affiliativeness (AF) dimension of temperament make more conceptual level responses of executive functions. The correlation coefficient of total number of correct responses of executive functions and Affiliativeness (AF) dimension of temperament is 0.29, which is not significant. The correlation coefficient of perseverative responses of executive functions and Affiliativeness (AF) dimension of temperament is -0.28, the perseverative error responses and the non perseverative responses of executive functions and Affiliativeness(AF) dimension of temperament are -0.22. These correlation coefficients are not significant.

Objective 12: To find out the relation between temperament and certain selected executive functions among Students with Learning Disabilities.

H0 2: There will be no relation between the total temperament scores and certain selected executive functions among Students with Learning Disabilities.

Table 4.35: Correlation coefficient of total temperament scores and executive functions among students with Learning Disabilities (N=40)

Executive Functions	Temperament
Total number of correct responses	0.42**
Total number of error responses	-0.39*
Perseverative responses	-0.32*
Perseverative error response	-0.32*
Non perseverative response	-0.25
Conceptual level response	0.39*

**. Correlation is significant at the 0.01 level.

*. Correlation is significant at the 0.05 level.

Table 4.35 shows that the correlation coefficient of temperament and executive functions among Students with Learning Disabilities. The correlation coefficient of total number of correct responses of executive functions and temperament is 0.42, which is significant at 0.01 levels. Hence the null hypothesis is rejected. That means there is a positive relationship between temperament and the total number of correct response of executive functions. The correlation coefficient of total number of error responses of executive functions and temperament is -0.39, which is significant at 0.05 levels. That is, there is an inverse relationship between temperament and total number of error response. High temperament leads to low level of the total number of error response of executive functions and vice versa. The correlation coefficient of perseverative responses of executive functions and temperament is -0.32, which is significant at 0.05 levels. There is an inverse relationship of temperament and perseverative response of Students with Learning Disabilities. This means that, in the light of feedback of the examiner that the previous sorting principle is no longer correct, the Students with Learning Disabilities must inhibit the tendency to persist or perseverate with old principle. The correlation coefficient of perseverative error responses of executive functions and temperament is -0.32, which is significant at 0.05 levels. There is an inverse relationship of temperament and perseverative error response of Students with Learning Disabilities. The correlation coefficient of non perseverative response is -0.25. That is, there is no significant relationship between the temperament and non perseverative response of executive function. But in the case of conceptual level of response, the correlation coefficient of conceptual level of response of Students with Learning Disabilities is 0.39, which is significant at 0.05 levels. There is a positive relationship between temperament and conceptual level response of executive functions among Students with Learning Disabilities. The above detail clearly shows that there is a relationship between temperament and executive functions among Students with Learning Disabilities. Studies are shown that there is a relationship between temperament and executive functions. That there is a novel relationship between temperament and executive functions were found in the study of the interrelations among youth temperament, executive functions and externalizing behaviour (Latzman, 2009).

Objective 13: To find out the relation between dimensions of character and certain selected executive functions among Students with Learning Disabilities.

H0 3: There will be no relation between dimensions of character and certain selected executive functions among Students with Learning Disabilities.

Table 4.36: Correlation coefficient of Self-Directedness (SD) of character and executive functions among students with Learning Disabilities (N=40)

Executive Functions	Self-Directedness (SD)
Total number of correct responses	0.27
Total number of error responses	-0.41**
Perseverative responses	-0.19
Perseverative error response	-0.31
Non perseverative response	-0.28
Conceptual level response	0.14

**. Correlation is significant at the 0.01 level.

Table 4.36 shows that the correlation coefficient of Self-Directedness (SD) of character and executive functions among Students with Learning Disabilities. The correlation coefficient of Self-Directedness (SD) of character and the total number of correct response of executive function is 0.27, which shows the positive relationship and it is not significant. The coefficient of correlation of character between perseverative response, perseverative error response, and non perseverative response are -0.19,-0.31 and -0.28 respectively. All the coefficients ofexecutive functions are shows no significant relationship between Self-Directedness (SD) of character score and all are inverse relationship. The correlation coefficient between the Self-Directedness (SD) of character and the total number of error response is -0.41, which is significant at 0.01 levels. That is, the Students with Learning Disabilities have low self directedness leads make more error responses of executive functions. Hence the null hypothesis is rejected.

Table 4.37: Correlation coefficient of Cooperativeness (CO) of character and executive functions among students with Learning Disabilities (N=40)

Executive Functions	Cooperativeness (CO)
Total number of correct responses	0.16
Total number of error responses	-0.24
Perseverative responses	-0.21
Perseverative error response	-0.19
Non perseverative response	-0.15
Conceptual level response	0.07

Table 4.37 shows that the correlation coefficient of Cooperativeness (CO) of character and executive functions among Students with Learning Disabilities. From the above table, it is clear thatthe correlation coefficient of Cooperativeness (CO) of character and executive functions among Students with Learning Disabilities have no significant relationship. The correlation coefficient of Cooperativeness (CO) of character and the total number of correct response of executive function is 0.16, which shows the weak positive relationship and it is not significant. The coefficient of correlation Cooperativeness (CO) of character between total number of error response is -0.24. The coefficient of correlation of Cooperativeness (CO) of character between perseverative response is -0.21. The coefficient of correlation of Cooperativeness (CO) of character between perseverative error response is -0.19. The coefficient of correlation of Cooperativeness (CO) of character between non perseverative response and conceptual level response are -0.15 and 0.07 respectively. All these coefficients values shows a weak correlation and all are not significant at any level. It means that there is no significant relationship between Cooperativeness (CO) of character and executive functions among Students with Learning Disabilities. Hence the null hypothesis is accepted.

Table 4.38: Correlation coefficient of Self-Transcendence (ST) of character and executive functions among students with Learning Disabilities (N=40)

Executive Functions	Self-Transcendence (ST)
Total number of correct responses	0.14
Total number of error responses	-0.18
Perseverative responses	0.14
Perseverative error response	0.07
Non perseverative response	-0.25
Conceptual level response	0.17

Table 4.38 shows that the correlation coefficient of Self-Transcendence (ST) of character and executive functions among Students with Learning Disabilities. The correlation coefficient of Self-Transcendence (ST) of character and the total number of correct response of executive function is 0.14. The coefficient of correlation Self-Transcendence (ST) of character between total number of error response is -0.18. The coefficient of correlation of Self-Transcendence (ST) of character between perseverative response is 0.14. The coefficient of correlation of Self-Transcendence (ST) of character between perseverative error response is 0.07. The coefficient of correlation of Self-Transcendence (ST) of character between non perseverative response and conceptual level response are -0.25 and 0.17 respectively. It is clear thatthe

correlation coefficient of Self-Transcendence (ST) of character and executive functions among Students with Learning Disabilities have no significant relationship. And also there is a relationship between Self-Transcendence (ST) of character and executive functions among Students with Learning Disabilities. Hence the null hypothesis is accepted.

Objective 14: To find out the relation between character and certain selected executive functions among Students with Learning Disabilities.

H0 4: There will be no relation between the total character scores and certain selected executive functions among Students with Learning Disabilities.

Table 4.39: Correlation coefficient of total character scores and executive functions among students with Learning Disabilities (N=40)

Executive Functions	Character
Total number of correct responses	0.21
Total number of error responses	-0.34*
Perseverative responses	-0.13
Perseverative error response	-0.19
Non perseverative response	-0.27
Conceptual level response	0.15

*. Correlation is significant at the 0.05 level.

Table 4.39 shows that the correlation coefficient of character and executive functions among Students with Learning Disabilities. The correlation coefficient of character and the total number of correct response of executive function is 0.21, which shows the positive relationship and it is not significant. The coefficient of correlation of character between perseverative response, perseverative error response, and non perseverative response are -0.13,-0.19 and -0.27 respectively. All the coefficients of executive functions are shows no significant relationship between character score and all are inverse relationship. The correlation coefficient between the character and the total number of error response is -0.34, which is significant at 0.05 level. Hence the null hypothesis is rejected. It means that the low scores of character of the Students with Learning Disabilities have more tendencies to make error responses. Many studies found that the character dimensions of self directedness and self transcendence were significantly associated with working memory, set shifting tasks, and complex cognitive processes including insight learning (Cassimjee & Murphy, 2010, Boeker *et al.*, 2006, Bergvall *et al.*, 2003).

Objective 15: To find out the relation between dimensions of temperament and certain selected executive functions among Students without Learning Disabilities.

H0 5: There will be no relation between dimensions of temperament and certain selected executive functions among Students without Learning Disabilities.

Table 4.40: Correlation coefficient of the Effortful Control (EC) of temperament and executive functions among students without Learning Disabilities (N=40)

Executive Functions	Effortful Control (EC)
Total number of correct responses	0.41**
Total number of error responses	-0.33*
Perseverative responses	-0.29
Perseverative error response	-0.29
Non perseverative response	-0.27
Conceptual level response	0.35*

**. Correlation is significant at the 0.01 level.

*. Correlation is significant at the 0.05 level.

Table 4.40 shows that the correlation coefficient of the Effortful Control (EC) of temperament and executive functions among Students without Learning Disabilities. The correlation coefficient of total number of correct responses of executive functions and Effortful Control (EC) of temperament is 0.41, which is significant at 0.01 levels. That means there is a moderately strong positive relationship between Effortful Control (EC) of temperament and the total number of correct response of executive functions. That is the students who have high in any areas of the Effortful Control (EC) of temperament like; attention, inhibitory control and activation control make more correct response. The correlation coefficient of total number of error responses of executive functions and Effortful Control (EC) of temperament is -0.33, which is also significant at 0.05 levels. That is there is a negative relationship betweenthe total number of error responses of executive functions and Effortful Control (EC) of temperament. That is the Students without Learning Disability have high Effortful Control (EC) of temperament leads to decrease in the total number of error responses of executive functions. Both the correlation coefficient of perseverative responses and perseverative error responses of executive functions and Effortful Control (EC) of temperament shows same coefficients, that is -0.29. Both arenot significant at any levels. The correlation coefficient of non-perseverative response is -0.27. That is, there is no significant relationship between the temperament and non perseverative response of executive function. But in the case of conceptual level of response, the correlation coefficient of conceptual level of response of Students without Learning Disabilities is 0.35, which is significant at 0.05 levels. There is a positive relationship between Effortful

Control (EC) of temperament and conceptual level response of executive functions among Students without Learning Disabilities. The above detail clearly shows that there is a significant relationship between Effortful Control (EC) of temperament and executive functions among Students without Learning Disabilities. Hence the null hypothesis is rejected.

Table 4.41: Correlation coefficient of the Surgency (S) of temperament and executive functions among students without Learning Disabilities (N=40)

Executive Functions	Surgency (S)
Total number of correct responses	0.26
Total number of error responses	-0.25
Perseverative responses	-0.26
Perseverative error response	-0.24
Non perseverative response	-0.17
Conceptual level response	0.24

Table 4.41 shows that the correlation coefficient of the Surgency (S) of temperament and executive functions among Students without Learning Disabilities. The correlation coefficients of total number of correct responses, error responses, perseverative response, perseverative error response, non-perseverative response and conceptual level responses with Surgency (S) of temperament are 0.26, -0.25, -0.26, -0.24, -0.17 and 0.24 respectively. From the table which is clear that the correlation coefficient of executive functions and Surgency (S) of temperament is not significant as well as show the weak correlations. Hence the null hypothesis is accepted.

Table 4.42: Correlation coefficient of the Negative Affect (NA) of temperament and executive functions among students without Learning Disabilities (N=40)

Executive Functions	Negative Affect (NA)
Total number of correct responses	0.06
Total number of error responses	0.44
Perseverative responses	-0.03
Perseverative error response	0.10
Non perseverative response	0.003
Conceptual level response	0.07

Table 4.42 shows that the correlation coefficient of the Negative Affect (NA) of temperament and executive functions among Students without Learning Disabilities. From the table which is clear that there is a no significant

correlation between the Negative Affect (NA) of temperament and executive functions among Students without Learning Disabilities. The values only shows that the weak correlations. The correlation coefficient of total number of correct responses and Negative Affect (NA) of temperament is 0.06. The correlation coefficient of total number of error responses and Negative Affect (NA) of temperament is 0.44. The coefficient of perseverative responses and Negative Affect (NA) of temperament is -0.03 and perseverative error responsesof executive functions and Negative Affect (NA) of temperament is 0.10. In the case of non-perseverative response, and conceptual level responses with Negative Affect (NA) of temperament are 0.003 and 0.07 respectively. Hence the null hypothesis accepted.

Table 4.43: Correlation coefficient of the Affiliativeness (AF) of temperament and executive functions among students without Learning Disabilities (N=40)

Executive Functions	Affiliativeness (AF)
Total number of correct responses	0.07
Total number of error responses	-0.04
Perseverative responses	0.05
Perseverative error response	0.07
Non perseverative response	-0.09
Conceptual level response	0.24

Table 4.43 shows that the correlation coefficient of the Affiliativeness (AF) of temperament and executive functions among Students without Learning Disabilities. From the table which is clear that there is a no significant correlation between the Affiliativeness (AF) of temperament and executive functions among Students without Learning Disabilities. The values only shows that the weak correlations. The correlation coefficient of total number of correct responses and Affiliativeness (AF) of temperament is 0.07. The correlation coefficient of total number of error responses and Affiliativeness (AF) of temperament is -0.04. The coefficient of perseverative responses and Affiliativeness (AF) of temperament is 0.05 and perseverative error responses of executive functions and Affiliativeness (AF) of temperament is 0.07.In the case of non-perseverative response, and conceptual level responses with Negative Affect (NA)of temperament are -0.09 and 0.24 respectively. Hence the null hypothesis accepted.

Objective 16: To find out the relation between temperament and certain selected executive functions among Students without Learning Disabilities.

H0 6: There will be no relation between the total temperament scores and certain selected executive functions among Students without Learning Disabilities.

Table 4.44: Correlation coefficient of total temperament scores and executive functions among students without Learning Disabilities (N=40)

Executive Functions	Temperament
Total number of correct responses	0.44**
Total number of error responses	-0.30
Perseverative responses	-0.29
Perseverative error response	-0.17
Non perseverative response	-0.29
Conceptual level response	0.49**

**. Correlation is significant at the 0.01 level.

*. Correlation is significant at the 0.05 level.

Table 4.44 shows that the correlation coefficient of temperament and executive functions among Students without Learning Disabilities. There is a significant relationship between temperament, total number of correct response and conceptual level response of executive functions. The correlation coefficient of temperament and total correct response of executive function is 0.44 and conceptual level response is 0.49, which shows a positive correlation. High temperament leads to high level of the total number of correct and conceptual level responses of executive functions and vice versa. According to Bergvall *et al.* (2003) many executive functions and temperament dimensions involve the prefrontal cortex. The prefrontal cortex and its other associated cortical areas are involved with planning, abstraction, attention and working memory tasks, which can be classified under executive functioning (Dennison, 2012, Cassimjee & Murphy, 2010). One such study (Martel *et al.*, 2008) showed that executive function task performance (response inhibition, response time variability, in adolescents also set-shifting) was related to effortful control as rated by parents, but not to reactive control (Drechsler *et al.*, 2015). The coefficient of correlation of temperament and the total number of error response is -0.30, which is not significant and shows a moderate negative relationship. The correlation coefficient of temperament and perseverative response is -0.29, which is again not significant between temperament of students without learning disabilities and it is a relationship between the factors. The correlation of temperament and perseverative error response of executive function is -0.17, it clearly shows that there is negligible relationship between the factors. The correlation coefficient of temperament and non perseverative response is -0.29, there also no significant relationship between the character dimension. Hence the null hypothesis is rejected.

Objective 17: To find out the relation between dimensions of character and certain selected executive functions among Students without Learning Disabilities.

H0 7: There will be no relation between dimensions of character and certain selected executive functions among Students without Learning Disabilities.

Table 4.45: Correlation coefficient of Self-Directedness (SD) of character and executive functions among students without Learning Disabilities (N=40)

Executive Functions	Self-Directedness (SD)
Total number of correct responses	0.22
Total number of error responses	-0.27
Perseverative responses	0.01
Perseverative error response	-0.04
Non perseverative response	-0.32*
Conceptual level response	0.08

*. Correlation is significant at the 0.05 level.

Table 4.45 shows that the correlation coefficient of Self-Directedness (SD) of character and executive functions among Students without Learning Disabilities. The correlation coefficient of Self-Directedness (SD) of character and the total number of correct response of executive function is 0.22, which shows the positive relationship and it is not significant. The coefficient of correlation of Self-Directedness (SD) of character between total numbers of error response perseverative response is -0.27, which shows a weak negative relationship. The coefficient of correlation of Self-Directedness (SD) of character between perseverative error response, perseverative error response and conceptual level response are 0.01, -0.04 and 0.08 respectively, which are also not significant. The correlation coefficient between theSelf-Directedness (SD) of character and the non perseverative error response is -0.32, which is significant at 0.05 levels. That is, the Students without Learning Disabilities have low self directedness leads make more non perseverative error responses of executive functions. Hence the null hypothesis is rejected.

Table 4.46: Correlation coefficient of Cooperativeness (CO) of character and executive functions among students without Learning Disabilities (N=40)

Executive Functions	Cooperativeness (CO)
Total number of correct responses	-0.03
Total number of error responses	0.09
Perseverative responses	-0.16
Perseverative error response	-0.14
Non perseverative response	0.18
Conceptual level response	0.08

Table 4.46 shows that the correlation coefficient of Cooperativeness (CO) of character and executive functions among Students without Learning Disabilities. From the above table, it is clear that the correlation coefficient of Cooperativeness (CO) of character and executive functions among Students with Learning Disabilities have no significant relationship. The correlation coefficient of Cooperativeness (CO) of character and the total number of correct response of executive function is -0.03, which shows the weak negative relationship and it is not significant. The coefficient of correlation Cooperativeness (CO) of character between total number of error response is 0.09. The coefficient of correlation of Cooperativeness (CO) of character between perseverative response is -0.16. The coefficient of correlation of Cooperativeness (CO) of character between perseverative error response is -0.14. The coefficient of correlation of Cooperativeness (CO) of character between non perseverative response and conceptual level response are, 0.18and 0.08 respectively. All these coefficients values shows a weak correlation and all are not significant. It means that there is no significant relationship between Cooperativeness (CO) of character and executive functions among Students without Learning Disabilities. Hence the null hypothesis is accepted.

Table 4.47: Correlation coefficient of Self-Transcendence (ST) of character and executive functions among students without Learning Disabilities (N=40)

Executive Functions	Self-Transcendence (ST)
Total number of correct responses	0.09
Total number of error responses	-0.12
Perseverative responses	-0.12
Perseverative error response	-0.15
Non perseverative response	-0.06
Conceptual level response	0.27

Table 4.47 shows that the correlation coefficient of Self-Transcendence (ST) of character and executive functions among Students without Learning Disabilities. The correlation coefficient of Self-Transcendence (ST) of character and the total number of correct response of executive function is 0.09. The coefficient of correlation Self-Transcendence (ST) of character between total number of error response is -0.12. The coefficient of correlation of Self-Transcendence (ST) of character between perseverative response is -0.12. The coefficient of correlation of Self-Transcendence (ST) of character between perseverative error response is -0.15. The coefficient of correlation of Self-Transcendence (ST) of character between non perseverative response and conceptual level response are -0.06 and 0.27 respectively. It is clear thatthe

correlation coefficient of Self-Transcendence (ST) of character and executive functions among Students without Learning Disabilities have no significant relationship. And also there is a weak relationship between Self-Transcendence (ST) of character and executive functions among Students without Learning Disabilities. Hence the null hypothesis is accepted.

Objective 18: To find out the relation between character and certain selected executive functions among Students without Learning Disabilities.

H0 8: There will be no relation between the total character scores and certain selected executive functions among Students without Learning Disabilities

Table 4.48: Correlation coefficient of total character scores and executive functions among students without Learning Disabilities (N=40)

Executive Functions	Character
Total number of correct responses	0.14
Total number of error responses	-0.08
Perseverative responses	-0.21
Perseverative error response	-0.20
Non perseverative response	0.01
Conceptual level response	0.15

Table 4.48 shows that the correlation coefficient of character and executive functions among Students without Learning Disabilities. The correlation coefficient of character and total number of correct response is 0.14; total number of error response is -0.08, perseverative response is -0.21, perseverative error response is -0.20, non perseverative response is 0.01 and conceptual level response is 0.15. The correlation coefficients of character and executive functions of Students without Learning Disabilities are weak. Hence the null hypothesis is accepted. Drechsler *et al* (2015), results of the study shows that the character scales were even less clearly attributable to either one of the two Behavioural Rating Inventory of Executive Function (BRIEF) main indices than the temperament scales among children with ADHD and clinical controls.

Objective 19: To compare the dimensions of temperament among Students with Learning Disabilities and without Learning Disabilities.

H0 9: There will be no significant difference in dimensions of temperament between Students with Learning Disabilities and without Learning Disabilities.

Table 4.49: The total sample, Mean, Standard Deviation (SD) & 't' value of the Effortful Control (EC) of temperament among students with and without Learning Disabilities

	Group	N	Mean	Standard Deviation	't'
Effortful Control (EC)	Students with Learning Disabilities	40	30.93	12.75	9.01**
	Students without Learning Disabilities	40	52.43	8.07	

** Significant at 0.01 level.

Table 4.49 shows the total sample (N), mean, standard deviation and 't' value of the Effortful Control (EC) of temperament among Students with and without Learning Disabilities. The total sample of Students with Learning Disabilities is 40 and without Learning Disabilities is 40. The mean score of the Students with Learning Disabilities is 30.93 and without Learning Disabilities is 52.43. The standard deviation of the Students with Learning Disabilities is 12.75 and Students without Learning Disabilities is 8.07. The obtained 't' value of the temperament among Students with and without Learning Disabilities are 9.01. Which is highly significant at 0.01 level. Hence the null hypothesis is rejected. The value shows that the Effortful Control (EC) of temperament scores of Students with Learning Disabilities lower than the Students without Learning Disabilities. The temperament predicted both high internalizing and low externalizing problems. Low Effortful Control (EC) is a consistent and strong predictor of externalizing problems and a less strong predictor of internalizing problems. Highly negative children will be show less problems when they have higher EC (Rothbart, 2007).

Table 4.50: The total sample, Mean, Standard Deviation (SD) & 't' value of the Surgency (S) of temperament among students with and without Learning Disabilities

	Group	N	Mean	Standard Deviation	't'
Surgency (S)	Students With Learning Disabilities	40	35.00	8.70	2.44*
	Students without Learning Disabilities	40	39.13	6.20	

* Significant at 0.05 level.

Table 4.50 shows the total sample (N), mean, standard deviation and 't' value of the Surgency (S) of temperament among Students with and without Learning Disabilities. The total sample of Students with Learning Disabilities is 40 and without Learning Disabilities is 40. The mean score of the Students with Learning Disabilities is 35.00 and without Learning Disabilities is 39.13. The standard deviation of the Students with Learning Disabilities is 8.70 and Students without Learning Disabilities is 6.02. The obtained 't' value of the temperament among Students with and without Learning Disabilities are 2.44. This is significant at 0.05level. Hence the null hypothesis is rejected. The value shows that the Surgency (S) of temperament scores of Students with Learning Disabilities lower than the Students without Learning Disabilities.

Table 4.51: The total sample, Mean, Standard Deviation (SD) & 't' value of the Negative Affect (NA) of temperament among students with and without Learning Disabilities

	Group	N	Mean	Standard Deviation	't'
Negative Affect (NA)	Students With Learning Disabilities	40	50.35	13.53	1.58
	Students without Learning Disabilities	40	46.10	10.39	

Table 4.51 shows the total sample (N), mean, standard deviation and 't' value of the Negative Affect (NA) of temperament among Students with and without Learning Disabilities. The total sample of Students with Learning Disabilities is 40 and without Learning Disabilities is 40. The mean score of the Students with Learning Disabilities is 50.35 and without Learning Disabilities is 46.10. The standard deviation of the Students with Learning Disabilities is 13.53 and Students without Learning Disabilities is 10.39. The obtained 't' value of the temperament among Students with and without Learning Disabilities are 1.58, which is not significant. Hence the null hypothesis is accepted. The value shows that there will be no significant difference between Negative Affect (NA) of temperament among Students with and without Learning Disabilities.

Table 4.52: The total sample, Mean, Standard Deviation (SD) & 't' value of the Affiliativeness (AF) of temperament among students with and without Learning Disabilities

	Group	N	Mean	Standard Deviation	't'
Affiliativeness (AF)	Students with Learning Disabilities	40	33.08	6.38	0.99
	Students without Learning Disabilities	40	34.48	6.34	

Table 4.52 shows the total sample (N), mean, standard deviation and 't' value of the Affiliativeness (AF) of temperament among Students with and without Learning Disabilities. The total sample of Students with Learning Disabilities is 40 and without Learning Disabilities is 40. The mean score of the Students with Learning Disabilities is 33.08 and without Learning Disabilities is 34.48. The standard deviation of the Students with Learning Disabilities is 6.38 and Students without Learning Disabilities is 6.34. The obtained 't' value of the temperament among Students with and without Learning Disabilities are 0.99, which is not significant. Hence the null hypothesis is accepted. The value shows that there will be no significant difference between Affiliativeness (AF) of temperament among Students with and without Learning Disabilities.

Objective 20: To compare the temperament among Students with Learning Disabilities and without Learning Disabilities.

H0 10: There will be no significant difference in the total temperament scores between Students with Learning Disabilities and without Learning Disabilities.

Table 4.53: The total sample, Mean, Standard Deviation (SD) & 't' value of the total temperament score among students with and without Learning Disabilities

	Group	N	Mean	Standard Deviation	't'
Total Temperament score	Students With Learning Disabilities	40	149.35	14.54	7.27**
	Students without Learning Disabilities	40	172.12	13.48	

** Significant at 0.01 level.

Table 4.53 shows the total sample (N), mean, standard deviation and 't' value of the temperament among Students with and without Learning Disabilities. The total sample of Students with Learning Disabilities is 40 and without Learning Disabilities is 40. The mean score of the Students with Learning Disabilities is 149.35 and without Learning Disabilities are 172.12. The standard deviation of the Students with Learning Disabilities is 14.54 and Students without Learning Disabilities is 13.48. The obtained 't' value of the temperament among Students with and without Learning Disabilities is 7.27. Which is highly significant at 0.01 level. Hence the null hypothesis is rejected. The value shows that the temperament scores of Students with Learning Disabilities lower than the Students without Learning Disabilities. Temperament variability among individual has been ascribed to neuro physiological variations in brain functioning (Henderson & Waches, 2007).

Objective 21: To compare the dimensions of character among Students with Learning Disabilities and without Learning Disabilities.

H0 11: There will be no significant difference in dimensions of character between Students with Learning Disabilities and without Learning Disabilities.

Table 4.54: The total sample, Mean, Standard Deviation(SD) & 't' value of the Self-Directedness (SD) of character among students with and without Learning Disabilities

	Group	N	Mean	Standard Deviation	't'
Self-Directedness (SD)	Students With Learning Disabilities	40	31.65	5.66	6.31**
	Students without Learning Disabilities	40	39.68	5.71	

** Significant at 0.01 level.

Table 4.54 shows the total sample (N), mean, standard deviation and 't' value of the Self-Directedness (SD) of character among Students with and without Learning Disabilities. The total sample of Students with Learning Disabilities is 40 and without Learning Disabilities is 40. The mean score of the Students with Learning Disabilities is 31.65 and without Learning Disabilities is 39.68. The standard deviation of the Students with Learning Disabilities is 5.66 and Students without Learning Disabilities is 5.71. The obtained 't' value of the Self-Directedness (SD) of character among Students with and without Learning Disabilities is 6.31. Which is highly significant at 0.01 level. Hence the null hypothesis is rejected. The value shows that the Self-Directedness (SD) of character scores of Students with Learning Disabilities lower than the Students without Learning Disabilities. In a Korean study shows that children with ADHD showed higher scores on Novelty Seeking and lower scores on the Self Directedness (SD) compared with controls (Yoo *et al.*, 2006, Cho, Kim, *et al.*, 2009, Purper- Ouakil *et al.*, 2010).

Table 4.55: The total sample, Mean, Standard Deviation (SD) & 't' value of the Cooperativeness (CO) of character among students with and without Learning Disabilities

	Group	N	Mean	Standard Deviation	't'
Cooperativeness (CO)	Students With Learning Disabilities	40	32.33	5.56	6.69**
	Students without Learning Disabilities	40	41.58	6.76	

** Significant at 0.01 level.

Table 4.55 shows the total sample (N), mean, standard deviation and 't' value of the Cooperativeness (CO) of character among students with and without learning disabilities. The total sample of students with learning disabilities is 40 and without learning disabilities is 40. The mean score of the students with learning disabilities is 32.33 and without learning disabilities is 41.58. The standard deviation of the students with learning disabilities is 5.56 and students without learning disabilities is 6.76. The obtained 't' value of the Cooperativeness (CO) of character among Students with and without Learning Disabilities is 6.69, which is highly significant at 0.01 level. Hence the null hypothesis is rejected. The value shows that the Cooperativeness (CO) of character scores of Students with Learning Disabilities lower than the Students without Learning Disabilities. Study shows that children with ADHD showed higher scores on Novelty Seeking and lower scores on the Cooperativeness (CO) compared with controls (Yoo *et al.*, 2006, Kerekes *et al.*, 2013).

Table 4.56: The total sample, Mean, Standard Deviation (SD) & 't' value of the Self-Transcendence (ST) of character among students with and without Learning Disabilities

	Group	N	Mean	Standard Deviation	't'
Self-Transcendence (ST)	Students with Learning Disabilities	40	16.18	4.55	3.68**
	Students without Learning Disabilities	40	19.68	3.92	

** Significant at 0.01 level.

Table 4.56 shows the total sample (N), mean, standard deviation and 't' value of the Self-Transcendence (ST) of character among Students with and without Learning Disabilities. The total sample of Students with Learning Disabilities is 40 and without learning disabilities are 40. The mean score of the Students with Learning Disabilities is 16.18 and without Learning Disabilities is 19.68. The standard deviation of the Students with Learning Disabilities is 4.55 and Students without Learning Disabilities are 3.92. The obtained 't' value of the Self-Transcendence (ST) of character among Students with and without Learning Disabilities is 3.68, which is highly significant at 0.01 level. Hence the null hypothesis is rejected. The value shows that the Self-Transcendence (ST) of character scores of Students with Learning Disabilities lower than the Students without Learning Disabilities. Higher Self-Transcendence (ST) scores of non clinical individuals may reflect a tolerance for ambiguity and may be strong reliance on working memory and higher internal monitoring (Cassimjee & Murphy, 2010).

Objective 22: To compare the character among Students with Learning Disabilities and without Learning Disabilities.

H0 12: There will be no significant difference in the total character scores between Students with Learning Disabilities and without Learning Disabilities.

Table 4.57: The total sample, Mean, Standard Deviation (SD) & 't' value of the total character score among students with and without Learning Disabilities

	Group	N	Mean	Standard Deviation	't'
Total Character Score	Students with Learning Disabilities	40	80.15	12.96	6.42**
	Students without Learning Disabilities	40	98.63	12.78	

** Significant at 0.01 level.

Table 4.57 shows the total sample(N), mean, standard deviation and 't' value of the total score of character among Students with and without Learning Disabilities. The total sample of Students with Learning Disabilities is 40 and without Learning Disabilities is 40. The mean score of the Students with Learning Disabilities is 80.15 and without Learning Disabilities is98.63. The standard deviation of the Students with Learning Disabilities is 12.96 and Students without Learning Disabilities are 12.78. The obtained 't' value of the total score of character among Students with and without Learning Disabilities is 6.42. Which is highly significant at 0.01 level. Hence the null hypothesis is rejected. The value shows that the character scores of Students with Learning Disabilities lower than the Students without Learning Disabilities. That is, they have low self directedness, cooperativeness and self transcendence of character scores than the Students without Learning Disabilities. According to Cassimjee & Murphy (2010), character development implies changes in the propositional memory system whereas temperament variation implies individual differences in procedural memory.

Objective 23: To compare certain selected executive functions among Students with Learning Disabilities and without Learning Disabilities.

H0 13: There will be no significant difference in certain selected executive functions between Students with Learning Disabilities and without Learning Disabilities.

Table 4.58: The total sample, Mean, Standard Deviation (SD) & 't' value of the total number of correct responses of students with and without Learning Disabilities

	Group	N	Mean	Standard Deviation	't'
Total Number of Correct Response	Students with Learning Disabilities	40	66.15	17.06	7.83**
	Students without Learning Disabilities	40	92.70	12.98	

** Significant at 0.01 level.

Table 4.58 shows the total sample (N), Mean, Standard deviation and "t" value and total number of correct responses of Students with and without Learning Disabilities. The 't' value obtained is 7.83, which is highly significant at 0.01 level. There is a significant difference in total number of correct responses of with and without Learning Disabilities. Hence the null hypothesis is rejected. The Student without Learning Disabilities makes more correct responses than the Students with Learning Disabilities. This means that the Students with Learning Disabilities fail to maintain correct sorting principles. The patients with frontal lesions demonstrated difficulties in self-control and in attentional shifting (Jurado & Rosselli, 2007; Golberg, 2001; Lezak *et al.*, 2004).

Table 4.59: The total sample, Mean, Standard Deviation (SD) & 't' value of the total number of error responses of students with and without Learning Disabilities

	Group	N	Mean	Standard Deviation	't'
Total number of error responses	Students with Learning Disabilities	40	53.20	17.47	5.33**
	Students without Learning Disabilities	40	34.80	13.13	

** Significant at 0.01 level.

Table 4.59 Shows the total sample (N), Mean, Standard deviation (SD) and "t" value and total number of error responses of with and without Learning Disabilities. The 't' value obtained is 5.33, which is highly significant at 0.01 level. There is a significant difference in total number of error responses of with and without Learning Disabilities. Hence the null hypothesis is rejected. The Students with Learning Disabilities makes more error responses than the Students without Learning Disabilities. This means that the Students with Learning Disabilities have low level of planning and problem solving ability. According to Vygotsky (1962), offering strategies while children are actively engaged in problem solving results in improved in cognitive control, error detection and self-correction (Carlson, 2015; Berk, 1992; Rogoff, 1990).

Table 4.60: The total sample, Mean, Standard Deviation (SD) & 't' value of the perseverative responses of students with and without Learning Disabilities

	Group	N	Mean	Standard Deviation	't'
Perseverative Response	Students with Learning Disabilities	40	31.95	11.60	6.49**
	Students without Learning Disabilities	40	18.40	6.31	

** Significant at 0.01 level.

Table 4.60 Shows the total sample (N), Mean, Standard deviation (SD) and "t" value and perseverative responses of with and without Learning Disabilities. The 't' value obtained is 6.49, which is highly significant at 0.01 level. There is a significant difference in total number of perseverative responses of with and without Learning Disabilities. Hence the null hypothesis is rejected. The Students with Learning Disabilities makes more perseverative responses than the Students without Learning Disabilities. This means that the capacity of the Students with Learning Disabilities engage in logical analysis was impaired. They appeared to have difficulty with cognitive flexibility. Their thinking appeared to be extremely perseverative, and should they begin with an unsuccessful approach to a new problem or situation. They might well continue with that unsuccessful approach well beyond the point where others would seek alternative solutions. Findings shows that until children are able to reflect on a more complex rule system, then errors like perseveration in rule use will occur. Problems with set shifting and a decrease in category fluency appear to be other relevant change with age (Jurado & Rosselli, 2007).

Table 4.61: The total sample, Mean, Standard Deviation (SD) & 't' value of the perseverative error responses of students with and without Learning Disabilities

	Group	N	Mean	Standard Deviation	't'
Perseverative Error Response	Students with Learning Disabilities	40	28.28	9.90	7.02**
	Students without Learning Disabilities	40	15.40	6.05	

** Significant at 0.01 level.

Table 4.61 Shows the total sample (N), Mean, Standard deviation (SD) and "t" value and perseverative error responses of with and without Learning Disabilities. The 't' value obtained is 7.02 which is highly significant at 0.01 level. There is a significant difference in total number of perseverative error responses of with and without Learning Disabilities. Hence the null hypothesis is rejected. The Studentswith Learning Disabilities makes more perseverative error responses than the Students without Learning Disabilities. This means that Students with Learning Disabilities appeared to have difficulty with cognitive flexibility. Their thinking begins with an unsuccessful approach to a new problem or situation. As the rules increase the complexity, however, the child will show more errors in flexibility ((Jurado & Rosselli, 2007). This ability improves considerably between the ages of 7 and 9 continues to improve until adolescence (Anderson, 2002; Zelazor & Frye, 1998).

Table 4.62: The total sample, Mean, Standard Deviation (SD) & 't' value of the non-perseverative error responses of students with and without Learning Disabilities

	Group	N	Mean	Standard Deviation	't'
Non Perseverative Error	Students with Learning Disabilities	40	24.70	14.54	1.94
	Students without Learning Disabilities	40	19.25	10.27	

Table 4.62 Shows the total sample (N), Mean, Standard deviation (SD) and "t" value and non-perseverative error responses of with and without Learning Disabilities. The 't' value obtained is 1.94 which is not significant. There is no significant difference in total number of non-perseverative error responses of with and without Learning Disabilities. Hence the null hypothesis is accepted.

Table 4.63: The total sample, Mean, Standard Deviation (SD) & 't' value of the conceptual level responses of students with and without Learning Disabilities

	Group	N	Mean	Standard Deviation	't'
Conceptual Level Response	Students with Learning Disabilities	40	35.60	15.69	9.04**
	Students without Learning Disabilities	40	69.78	18.03	

** Significant at 0.01 level.

Table 4.63 Shows the total sample (N), Mean, Standard deviation (SD) and "t" value and conceptual level responses of with and without Learning Disabilities. The 't' value obtained is 9.04, which is highly significant at 0.01 level. There is a significant difference in conceptual level responses of with and without Learning Disabilities. Hence the null hypothesis is rejected. The Students without Learning Disabilities makes more conceptual level responses than the students with Learning Disabilities. The Students without Learning Disabilities are able to retain new information and maintain recent information. Difficulties experienced by children with learning disabilities in concept formation are felt to reflect inefficient brain processing and patterning or impairment in the capacity to scan and screen out stimuli selectively. Such a view is based on a neurological model (Parucka, 1972).

Objective 24: To compare the dimensions of temperament with respect to age.

H0 14: There will be no significant difference in dimensions of temperament with respect to age.

Table 4.64: The total sample, Mean, Standard Deviation & 't' value of the Effortful Control (EC) of temperament among the age group of students with and without Learning Disabilities

	Age Group	N	Mean	Standard Deviation	't'
Effortful Control (EC)	13-14	47	40.74	14.48	0.65
	15-16	33	43	16.18	

Table 4.64 shows the total sample(N), mean, standard deviation and 't' value of the Effortful Control (EC) of temperament among the age group of Students with and without Learning Disabilities. The total sample of the age group 13-14 is 47 and the age group of 15-16 is 33. The mean score of the age group 13-14 is 40.74 and the age group of 15-16 is 43. The standard deviation of the age group 13-14 is 14.48 and the age group of 15-16 is 16.18. The obtained 't' value of the temperament among the age group of Students with and without Learning Disabilities is 0.65, which is not significant. Hence the null hypothesis is accepted. The value shows that the Effortful Control (EC) of temperament scores of the age group of Students with and without Learning Disabilities has no significant difference.

Table 4.65: The total sample, Mean, Standard Deviation and 't' value of the Surgency (S) of temperament among the age group of students with and without Learning Disabilities

	Age Group	N	Mean	Standard Deviation	't'
Surgency (S)	13-14	47	37.74	7.88	0.55
	15-16	33	36.48	7.75	

Table 4.65 shows the total sample (N), mean, standard deviation and 't' value of the Surgency (S) of temperament among the age group of Students with and without Learning Disabilities. The total sample of the age group 13-14 is 47 and the age group of 15-16 is 33. The mean score of the age group 13-14 is 37.74 and the age group of 15-16 is 36.48. The standard deviation of the age group 13-14 is 7.88 and the age group of 15-16 is 7.75. The obtained 't' value of the temperament among the age group of Students with and without Learning Disabilities are 0.55, which is not significant. Hence the null hypothesis is accepted. The value shows that the Surgency (S) of temperament scores of the age group of Students with and without Learning Disabilities has no significant difference.

Table 4.66: The total sample, Mean, Standard Deviation & 't' value of the Negative Affect (NA) of temperament among the age group of students with and without Learning Disabilities

	Age Group	N	Mean	Standard Deviation	't'
Negative Affect (NA)	13-14	47	48.87	11.18	0.57
	15-16	33	47.30	13.59	

Table 4.66 shows the total sample (N), mean, standard deviation and 't' value of the Negative Affect (NA) of temperament among the age group of Students with and without Learning Disabilities. The total sample of the age group 13-14 is 47 and the age group of 15-16 is 33. The mean score of the age group 13-14 is 48.87 and the age group of 15-16 is 47.30. The standard deviation of the age group 13-14is 11.18 and the age group of 15-16 is 13.59. The obtained 't' value of the temperament among the age group of Students with and without Learning Disabilities is 0.57, which is not significant. Hence the null hypothesis is accepted. The value shows that the Negative Affect (NA) of temperament scores of the age group of Students with and without Learning Disabilities has no significant difference.

Table 4.67: The total sample, Mean, Standard Deviation & 't' value of the Affiliativeness (AF) of temperament among the age group of students with and without Learning Disabilities

	Age Group	N	Mean	Standard Deviation	't'
Affiliativeness (AF)	13-14	47	34.13	6.04	0.59
	15-16	33	33.27	6.85	

Table 4.67 shows the total sample (N), mean, standard deviation and 't' value of the Affiliativeness (AF) of temperament among the age group of Students with and without Learning Disabilities. The total sample of the age group 13-14 is 47 and the age group of 15-16 is 33. The mean score of the age

group 13-14 is 34.13 and the age group of 15-16 is 33.27. The standard deviation of the age group 13-14 is 6.04 and the age group of 15-16 is 6.85. The obtained 't' value of the temperament among the age group of Students with and without Learning Disabilities is 0.59, which is not significant. Hence the null hypothesis is accepted. The value shows that the Affiliativeness (AF) of temperament scores of the age group of Students with and without Learning Disabilities has no significant difference.

Objective 25: To compare the temperament with respect to age.

H0 15: There will be no significant difference in the total temperament scores with respect to age.

Table 4.68: The total sample, Mean, Standard Deviation & 't' value of the total temperament score among the age group of students with and without Learning Disabilities

	Age Group	N	Mean	Standard Deviation	't'
Total Temperament score	13-14	47	161.21	14.98	0.28
	15-16	33	160.06	21.92	

Table 4.68 shows the total sample (N), mean, standard deviation and 't' value of the total scoreofthetemperament among the age group of Students with and without Learning Disabilities. The total sample of the age group 13-14 is 47 and the age group of 15-16 is 33. The mean score of the age group 13-14 is 161.21 and the age group of 15-16 is 160.06. The standard deviation of the age group 13-14 is 14.98 and the age group of 15-16 is 21.92. The obtained 't' value of the temperament among the age group of Students with and without Learning Disabilities is 0.28, which is not significant. Hence the null hypothesis is accepted. The value shows that the total score of temperament of the age group of Students with and without Learning Disabilities has no significant difference.

Objective 26: To compare the dimensions of character with respect to age.

H0 16: There will be no significant difference in dimensions of character with respect to age.

Table 4.69: The total sample, Mean, Standard Deviation & 't' value of the Self-Directedness (SD) of character among the age group of students with and without Learning Disabilities

	Age Group	N	Mean	Standard Deviation	't'
Self-Directedness (SD)	13-14	47	36.53	6.50	1.34
	15-16	33	34.42	7.46	

Table 4.69 shows the total sample (N), mean, standard deviation and 't' value of the Self-Directedness (SD) of character amongthe age group students with and without learning disabilities. The total sample of students with learning disabilities is 47 and without learning disabilities is 33. The mean score of the age group 13-14 is 36.53 and the age group 15-16 is 34.42. The standard deviation of the age group 13-14 is 6.50 and the age group 15-16 is 7.46. The obtained 't' value of the Self-Directedness (SD) of character among the age group students with and without learning disabilities is 1.34, which is not significant. Hence the null hypothesis is accepted.

Table 4.70: The total sample, Mean, Standard Deviation & 't' value of the Cooperativeness (CO) of character among the age group students with and without Learning Disabilities

	Age Group	N	Mean	Standard Deviation	't'
Cooperativeness (CO)	13-14	47	38.23	5.99	1.80
	15-16	33	35.12	9.45	

Table 4.70 shows the total sample (N), mean, standard deviation and 't' value of the Cooperativeness (CO) of character among the age group of students with and without learning disabilities. The total sample of students with learning disabilities is 47 and without learning disabilities is 33. The mean score of the age group 13-14 is 38.23 and the age group 15-16 is 35.12. The standard deviation of the age group 13-14 is 5.99 and the age group 15-16 is 9.45. The obtained 't' value of the Cooperativeness (CO) of character amongthe age group students with and without learning disabilities is 1.80,which is not significant. Hence the null hypothesis is accepted.

Table 4.71: The total sample, Mean, Standard Deviation & 't' value of the Self-Transcendence (ST) of character among the age group of students with and without Learning Disabilities

	Age Group	N	Mean	Standard Deviation	't'
Self-Transcendence (ST)	13-14	47	19.04	4.33	2.71**
	15-16	33	16.33	4.50	

** Significant at 0.01 level.

Table 4.71 shows the total sample (N), mean, standard deviation and 't' value of the Self-Transcendence (ST) of character among the age group of students with and without learning disabilities. The total sample of the age group of 13-14 is 47 and the age group of 15-16 is 33. The mean score of the age group of 13-14 is 19.04 and the age group of 15-16 is 16.33. The standard deviation of the age group of 13-14 is 4.33 and the age group of 15-16 is 4.50. The obtained 't' value of the Self-Transcendence (ST) of character amongthe age group of students with and without learning disabilities is 2.71, which is highly significant at 0.01 level. Hence the null hypothesis is rejected. The value shows that the Self-Transcendence (ST) of character scores of the age group of 13-14 is higher than the age group of 15-16.

Objective 27: To compare the character with respect to age.

H0 17: There will be no significant difference in the total character scores with respect to age.

Table 4.72: The total sample, Mean, Standard Deviation & 't' value of the total character score among the age group of students with and without Learning Disabilities

	Age Group	N	Mean	Standard Deviation	't'
Total Character Score	13-14	47	93.81	13.09	2.31*
	15-16	33	85.88	17.59	

* Significant at 0.05 level.

Table 4.72 shows the total sample (N), mean, standard deviation and 't' value of the total score of character among the age group of students with and without learning disabilities. The total sample of the age group 13-14 is 47 and the age group of 15-16 is 33. The mean score of the age group 13-14 is 93.81 and the age group of 15-16 is 85.88. The standard deviation of the students with learning disabilities is 13.09 and students without learning disabilities is 17.59. The obtained 't' value of the total score of character among the age group of students with and without learning disabilities is 2.31. Which is significant at 0.05 level. Hence the null hypothesis is rejected. The value shows that the character scores of the age group of 13-14 are higher than the age group of 15-16.

Objective 28: To compare the certain selected executive functions with respect to age.

H0 18: There will be no significant difference in certain selected executive functions with respect to age.

Table 4.73: The total sample, Mean, Standard Deviation & 't' value of the total number of correct responses of the age group of students with and without Learning Disabilities

	Age Group	N	Mean	Standard Deviation	't'
Total Number of Correct Response	13-14	47	79.49	18.49	0.13
	15-16	33	78.88	22.62	

Table 4.73 shows the total sample (N), Mean, Standard deviation and "t" value and total number of correct responses of the age group of Students with and without Learning Disabilities. The 't' value obtained is 0.13, which

is not significant. There is no significant difference in total number of correct responses of the age group between 13-14 and 15-16. Hence the null hypothesis is accepted.

Table 4.74: The total sample, Mean, Standard Deviation & 't' value of the total number of error responses of the age group of students with and without Learning Disabilities

	Age Group	N	Mean	Standard Deviation	't'
Total number of error responses	13-14	47	43.09	16.12	0.64
	15-16	33	45.69	20.57	

Table 4.74 shows the total sample (N), Mean, Standard deviation and "t" value and total number of error responses of the age group of the students with and without Learning Disabilities. The 't' value obtained is 0.64, which is not significant. There is no significant difference in total number of error responses of the age group between 13-14 and 15-16. Hence the null hypothesis is accepted.

Table 4.75: The total sample, Mean, Standard Deviation & 't' value of the perseverative responses of the age group of students with and without Learning Disabilities

	Age Group	N	Mean	Standard Deviation	't'
Perseverative Response	13-14	47	25.06	10.65	0.19
	15-16	33	25.58	13.13	

Table 4.75 shows the total sample (N), Mean, Standard deviation and "t" value and perseverative responses of the age group of Students with and without Learning Disabilities. The 't' value obtained is 0.19, which is not significant. There is no significant difference in perseverative responses of the age group between 13-14 and 15-16. Hence the null hypothesis is accepted.

Table 4.76: The total sample, Mean, Standard Deviation & 't' value of the perseverative error responses of the age group of students with and without Learning Disabilities

	Age Group	N	Mean	Standard Deviation	't'
Perseverative Error Response	13-14	47	21.64	9.75	0.34
	15-16	33	22.45	11.80	

Table 4.76 shows the total sample (N), Mean, Standard deviation and "t" value and perseverative error responses of the age group of student with and without Learning Disabilities. The 't' value obtained is 0.34, which

is not significant. There is no significant difference in perseverative error responses of the age group between 13-14 and 15-16. Hence the null hypothesis is accepted.

Table 4.77: The total sample, Mean, Standard Deviation & 't' value of the non-perseverative error responses of the age group of students with and without Learning Disabilities

	Age Group	N	Mean	Standard Deviation	't'
Non perseverative Error	13-14	47	21.19	11.14	0.68
	15-16	33	23.18	15.06	

Table 4.77 shows the total sample (N), Mean, Standard deviation and "t" value and non-perseverative error responses of the age group of student with and without Learning Disabilities. The 't' value obtained is 0.68 which is not significant. There is no significant difference in total number of non-perseverative error responses of the age group between 13-14 and 15-16. Hence the null hypothesis is accepted.

Table 4.78: The total sample, Mean, Standard Deviation & 't' value of the conceptual level responses of the age group of students with and without Learning Disabilities

	Group	N	Mean	Standard Deviation	't'
Conceptual Level Response	13-14	47	53.38	22.68	0.37
	15-16	33	51.33	26.35	

Table 4.78 shows the total sample (N), Mean, Standard deviation and "t" value and conceptual level responses of the age group of students with and without Learning Disabilities. The 't' value obtained is 0.37, which is not significant. There is no significant difference in conceptual level responses of the age group between 13-14 and 15-16. Hence the null hypothesis is accepted.

Objective 29: To compare the relationship of temperament and executive functions among Students with Learning Disabilities and without Learning Disabilities.

H0 19: There will be no relation between the correlation coefficient of total temperament scores and certain selected executive functions among Students with Learning Disabilities than that of Students without Learning Disabilities.

Table 4.79: Correlation coefficient of total temperament scores and executive functions comparison between students with Learning Disabilities and without Learning Disabilities (N=40)

Executive Functions	Temperament	
	Students with Learning Disabilities	Students without Learning Disabilities
Total number of correct responses	0.42**	0.44**
Total number of error responses	-0.39*	-0.30
Perseverative responses	-0.32*	-0.29
Perseverative error response	0.32*	-0.17
Non perseverative response	-0.25	-0.29
Conceptual level response	0.39*	0.49**

** Correlation is significant at the 0.01 level.

* Correlation is significant at the 0.05 level.

Table 4.79 shows that the correlation coefficient of temperament and executive functions comparison between Students with Learning Disabilities and Students without Learning Disabilities. From the table it is evident that the Students with Learning Disabilities have more significant link between the temperament and executive functions than that of the Students without Learning Disabilities. It means that the temperament dimensions such as effortful control, surgency and affiliativeness of Students with Learning Disabilities leads more problems in the multiple cognitive tasks such as the organized searching, abstract reasoning, the ability to initiate and stop actions, to monitor and change behaviour as needed, and to plan future behaviour when faced with novel tasks and situations. In the case of Students without Learning Disabilities, they have significant link to temperament with number of correct responses and conceptual level response only. Therefore the null hypothesis is rejected.

Objective 30: To compare the relationship of character and executive functions among Students with Learning Disabilities and without Learning Disabilities.

H0 20: There will be no relation between the correlation coefficient of total character scores and certain selected executive functions among Students with Learning Disabilities than that of Students without Learning Disabilities.

Table 4.80: Correlation coefficient of total character scores and executive functions comparison between students with Learning Disabilities and without Learning Disabilities (N=40)

Executive Functions	Character	
	Students with Learning Disabilities	Students without Learning Disabilities
Total number of correct responses	0.21	0.14
Total number of error responses	-0.34*	-0.08
Perseverative responses	-0.13	-0.21
Perseverative error response	-0.19	-0.20
Non perseverative response	-0.27	-0.01
Conceptual level response	0.15	0.15

* Correlation is significant at the 0.05 level.

Table 4.80 shows that the correlation coefficient of character and executive functions comparison between Students with Learning Disabilities and Students without Learning Disabilities. From the table shows that the Students with Learning Disabilities have only significant link between the character and error responses of executive functions, whereas the Students without Learning Disabilities have no significant link between character and executive functions. It means that the Students with Learning Disabilities have the environmental interactions and the self directedness such as, goal directedness, fluency of ideas, and sense of responsibility, self-congruence, and self-acceptance are adversely affecting their inherited cognitive issues whereas the Students without Learning Disabilities have not significantly linked each other. Therefore the null hypothesis is rejected.

DISCUSSION

The present study found that the temperament, character and executive functions among Students with and without Learning Disabilities. The study intended to find out the significant difference in the temperament, character and executive functions among Students with and without Learning Disabilities. The results of the study found that in the case of Students with Learning Disabilities have moderate positive correlation with the Effortful Control (EC) of temperament and the total number of correct response and conceptual level response of executive functions. This shows that the Students with Learning Disabilities attention process, inhibitory control and activation control over behaviours are play a supportive role in cognitive tasks and learning processes (Table 4.31). In the case of Surgency (S) of the temperament of Students with Learning Disabilities is inverse weak correlation to the perseverative responses and perseverative error response (Table 4.32). It means that the Students with Learning Disabilities have low scores in high intensity pleasure, shy and fear will lead to more in the light of the feedback that previous principle is no longer correct, the subjects must inhibit the tendency to persist with old principle. But in the case of Negative Affect (NA) of temperament among Students with Learning Disabilities shows no relationship between executive functions (Table 4.33) whereas the Affiliativeness (AF) of the temperament among Students with Learning Disabilities shows a negative weak correlation between total number of error responses and a moderate positive relationship between conceptual level responses. That is, the Students with Learning Disabilities have low scores in affiliation, perceptual sensitivity and pleasure sensitivity make more errors in their cognitive functions and learning. But high scores in this Affiliativeness (AF) make more conceptual level skills (Table 4.34). The table 4.35 shows that there is a moderate positive relationship in total temperament scores with the total number of correct response and weak positive relationship between conceptual level responses. In the case of the total error response, perseverative response, and perseverative error response of executive functions among Students with Learning Disabilities shows weak inverse relationship. The temperament has no significant relationship with the non perseverative response of executive functions among Students with Learning Disabilities. The temperament positively associated with the conceptual level response of executive functions among Students with Learning Disabilities. Among children with learning disabilities, temperament was more strongly related to teachability ratings than were student's cognitive abilities (Keogh, 1983). In the case of character, the Self Directedeness (SD) shows that there is a moderate inverse relationship with the total number of error response of executive functions among Students with Learning Disabilities than the other factors of executive functions (Table 4.36). This means that the Students with Learning Disabilities have low in goal directedness, fluency of ideas, sense of responsibility, self congruence, and self acceptance make more errors in their ability to initiate and stop activities, to monitor and change behaviour as required, and to plan future behavior. Whereas the other dimensions of character like, Cooperativeness (CO) (Table 4.37) and Self-Transcendence (ST) (Table 4.38) among Students with Learning Disabilities indicate no significant relationship with executive functions. In the case of total character scores and executive functions among Students with Learning Disabilities (Table 4.39) shows that there is a weak inverse significant relationship between the total number of error. That is low scores of character may lead more errors in their set of cognitive abilities that are control and regulate behaviours. Bergwall *et al.* (2003) and Boeker *et al.* (2006) found a significant association between Cloninger's character dimensions and neuropsychological performances. Character is believed to e environmentally influenced by cultural and social influences (Prosnick *et al.*, 2003).

On the other hand, in the case of Students without Learning Disabilities shows there is only significant association between Effortful Control (EC) of temperament and total number of correct response, error response and conceptual level response (Table 4.40). Which means that the high scores in attention, inhibitory and activation control leads high in conceptual level responses and correct responses in their cognitive skills, whereas the high scores in Effortful Control (EC) decreases to make errors also. But, the Surgency (S) (Table 4.41), Negative Affect (NA) (Table 4.42) and Affiliativeness (AF) (Table 4.43) does not show any significant relationships with executive function. The total temperament score (Table 4.44) among Students without Learning Disabilities indicates a moderate significant positive relationship between total number of correct response and conceptual responses. That is, the high inherited traits are making more ability to recognize the significance of unexpected situations and to make alternative plans rapidly when unusual events originate and hinder with normal routines. The study of genetic influences on temperament in young children is exciting because it supports research demonstrating that adult personality measures are heritable. Knowing that this begins early in childhood is important in understanding the entire development of personality (DiLalla & Jones, 2000). The Self Directedness (SD) shows that there is a weak inverse relationship with the non-perseverative response of executive functions among Students without Learning Disabilities than the other factors of executive functions (Table 4.45). This means that the high score of goal directedness, fluency of ideas, and sense of responsibility, self congruence, and self acceptance make decrease errors in their higher order functioning. But, in the case of Cooperativeness (CO) (Table 4.46), Self-Transcendence (ST) (Table 4.47) and total character score (Table 4.48) among Students without Learning Disabilities indicates no significant relationship with executive functions. The character dimensions involves the individual difference in higher cognitive functions such as self concepts about goals and values (Svrakic *et al.*, 2002, Dennison, 2012).

The study shows that there exists a difference in Effortful Control (EC) of temperament among Students with Learning Disabilities and Students without Learning Disabilities (Table 4.49). That is the Students with Learning Disabilities have lower in attention process, inhibitory control and activation control than Students without Learning Disabilities. The table 4.50 shows that there exists a difference in Surgency (S) of temperament among Students with and without Learning Disabilities. It also indicates that the Students with Learning Disabilities have low in high intensity pleasure than Students without Learning Disabilities. But in the case of Negative Affect (NA) (Table 4.51) and Affiliativeness (AF) (Table 4.52) of temperament among Students with Learning Disabilities and Students without Learning Disabilities shows no significant difference. That is both the Students with and without Learning Disabilities has no difference in the frustration, depressive mood, aggression, affiliation, pleasure sensitivity and perceptual sensitivity. Whereas, there exist a difference in total temperament score among Students with and without Learning Disabilities (Table 4.53). The Students without Learning Disabilities have high temperament scores than Students without Learning Disabilities. The study shows that there is a difference in all dimensions of character among Students with Learning Disabilities and Students without Learning Disabilities. That means there is a difference in Self-Directedness (SD) of character among Students with Learning Disabilities and Students without Learning Disabilities (Table 4.54). That is, Students with Learning Disabilities has low goal directedness, fluency of ideas, and sense of responsibility, self congruence, and self acceptance than Students without Learning Disabilities. The Cooperativeness (CO) of character among Students with and without Learning Disabilities shows a significant difference (Table 4.55). It explains the Students with Learning Disabilities has low social acceptance, empathy, helpfulness, compassion for others, and conscience than Students without Learning Disabilities. On the other hand, Students without Learning Disabilities have high in spirituality and fantasy than Students with Learning Disabilities (Table 4.56). The total character scores are low in Students with Learning Disabilities than Students without Learning Disabilities (Table 4.57). That is the Students with Learning Disabilities have low scores on character than compared to Students without Learning Disabilities. In the executive functions, there exists a difference in Students with Learning Disabilities and without Learning Disabilities. There is impairment in certain areas of executive functions among Students with Learning Disabilities compared to Students without Learning Disabilities. In the case of total number of correct responses (Table 4.58) the Students with Learning Disabilities has less correct responses than Students without Learning Disabilities and in the total number of error responses (Table 4.59), Students with Learning Disabilities make more errors and confusions. They need much more time to solve any type of problems, because they are not able to understand how these concepts are organized. The results shows that Students with Learning Disabilities have high perseveration, such as perseverative responses (Table 4.60) and perseverative error responses (Table 4.61) they had great difficulties in generating alternative problem solving approaches. Students with Learning Disabilities create less conceptual level responses (Table 4.63) than Students without Learning Disabilities. So they are impaired in their capacity to engage in logical analysis and form new concepts, and they appeared to have difficulty with cognitive flexibility. It is clear that the students with learning disabilities are facing variations in temperament, character and have impairment in executive functions than students without learning disability.

In the case of age group, the study shows that there is no significant difference in the dimensions of temperament like Effortful Control (EC) (Table 4.64), Surgency (S) (Table 4.65), Negative Affect (NA) (Table 4.66), Affiliativeness (AF) (Table 4.67) and total temperament scores (Table 4.68). Same as in the case of age group of Self-Directedness (SD) (Table 4.69) and Cooperativeness (CO) (Table 4.70). But, the study also shows that the age group of 13 to 14 shows high in spirituality and fantasy than with the age group of 15 to 16 (Table 4.71). The total character scores of age group 13 to 14 has high than with the age group of 15 to 16 (Table 4.72). Also the study shows that there is no significant difference in executive functions such as thetotal number of correct response (Table 4.73), total number of errors (Table 4.74), perseverative response (Table 4.75), perseverative error response (Table 4.76), non-perseverative response (Table 4.77) and the conceptual level response (Table 4.78). Importantly, the results of the study shows that the comparatively the Students with Learning Disabilities have more links between temperament and executive functions than that of Students without Learning Disabilities (Table 4.79). Also, the Students with Learning Disabilities have significant link between character and error response of the executive functions only, whereas the Students without Learning Disabilities have no significant relationship between these variables (Table 4.80). The results of the study concluded that the Students with and without Learning Disabilities have influenced between genetic and environmental dispositions to their cognitive flexibilities.

5

Findings, Summary and Conclusion

"A conclusion is the place where you get tired of thinking".

– Arthur Blouch

INTRODUCTION

The Students with Learning Disabilities have the problems in control and regulate their abilities, behaviour and academic performances. The present study was an attempt to assess the temperament, character and executive functions among Students with and without Learning Disabilities. To attain the objectives of the study, in the first phase was to develop the instrument, Early Adolescent Temperament and Character Inventory (EATCI) for measuring temperament and character. In the second phase, to assess the temperament, character and executive functions by using EATCI along with Wisconsin Card Sorting Test (WCST). This chapter outline the major findings, strengths and weakness, implications, suggestions and conclusions of study were discussed.

FINDINGS

1. There is a significant positive relationship between Effortful Control (EC) and the correct responses of executive functions among Students with Learning Disabilities. Hence the attentional process, inhibitory control and activation controls are inter related to their higher order cognitive capacities like strategic planning, organized searching, the application of external feedback to shift mental sets, and the inhibition of impulsive responses.
2. There is a significant positive relationship between Effortful Control (EC) and the conceptual level response of executive functions among Students with Learning Disabilities. This is the evidence of highattention process, inhibitory control and activation controls are influenced their conceptual process.

3. There is a significant negative relationship between Surgency (S) and the perseverative responses of executive functions among Students with Learning Disabilities. This means that the Surgency (S) scores inversely lead to make tendency to inhibit to persist or perseverate to old principles.
4. There is a significant negative relationship between Surgency (S) and the perseverative error responses of executive functions among Students with Learning Disabilities. It indicates that the low Surgency (S) factors like, high intensity pleasure, fear, and shyness leads to make high tendency to inhibit to persist or perseverate to error in old principles.
5. There is a significant negative relationship between Affiliativeness (AF) and the total number of error responses of executive functions among Students with Learning Disabilities. This means that the low Affiliativeness (AF) factors like, affiliation, perceptual sensitivity and pleasure sensitivity leads to high error in multiple cognitive operations.
6. There is a significant positive relationship between Affiliativeness (AF) and the conceptual level responses of executive functions among Students with Learning Disabilities. That is,the high level of Affiliativeness (AF) factors such as, affiliation, perceptual sensitivity and pleasure sensitivity lead high organized searching or conceptual level responses of executive functions.
7. There is a significant positive relationship between the temperament and the correct response of executive functions among Students with Learning Disabilities. This is because of the influence of the biologically based dispositions on their strategic planning, organized searching, the application of external feedback to shift mental sets, and the inhibition of impulsive responses.
8. There is a significant relationship between the temperament and the error response of executive functions among Students with Learning Disabilities. This means that the genetic traits inversely associated with the cognitive capabilities of Students with Learning Disabilities.
9. There is a negative relationship between thetemperament and the perseverative response of executive functions among Students with Learning Disabilities, which is also significant. Hence the temperament is negatively affects the cognitive flexibility of the Students with Learning Disabilities.
10. There is a significant negative relationship between the temperament and the perseverative error response of executive functions among Students with Learning Disabilities. From this it is clear that there is an inverse relationship between genetic dispositions of Students with Learning Disabilities and their thinking, with an unsuccessful approach to a new problem or situation.

11. There is a significant positive relationship between the temperament and the conceptual level response of executive functions among Students with Learning Disabilities. It shows that the low level of temperament of Students with Learning Disabilities leads their inability to retain new information and maintain recent information.
12. There is a significant inverse relationship between Self-Directedness (SD) and the total number of error responses of executive functions among Students with Learning Disabilities. It means that low score of goal directedness, fluency of ideas, and sense of responsibility, self congruence, and self acceptance leads to more error in multiple cognitive operations.
13. There is a significant negative relationship between character and the error response of executive functions among Students with Learning Disabilities. It shows that the Students with Learning Disabilities have low level of character creates more error responses. Because they can't adapt or understand the changes of the environment feedback.
14. There is a significant positive relationship between the Effortful Control (EC) and the correct responses of executive functions among Students without Learning Disabilities. That is the high Effortful Control (EC) like attention, inhibitory control and activation control, make more high cognitive functions which include strategic planning, organized searching, the application of external feedback to shift mental sets, and the inhibition of impulsive responses.
15. There is a significant negative relationship between Effortful Control (EC) and error responses of executive functions among Students without Learning Disabilities. Therefore, the low score of attention, inhibitory control and activation control, make more high error in cognitive functions which include strategic planning, organized searching, the application of external feedback to shift mental sets, and the inhibition of impulsive responses.
16. There is a significant positive relationship between Effortful Control (EC) and conceptual level responses of executive functions among Students without Learning Disabilities. That is, high Effortful Control (EC) like attention, inhibitory control and activation control leads to increased ability in organized searching.
17. There is a significant positive relationship betweentemperamentand the correct response of executive functions among Students without Learning Disabilities. This means that, the high genetic dispositions of Students without Learning Disabilities lead high performances in the executive functions.
18. There is a significant positive relationship betweentemperamentand the conceptual level response of executive functions among Students without

Learning Disabilities. It shows that the high level temperament of Students without Learning Disabilities leads their ability to retain new information and maintain recent information.

19. The Self-Directedness (SD) and non-perseverative responses of executive functions among Students without Learning Disabilities shows a significant inverse relationship. That means the low score of goal directedness, fluency of ideas, and sense of responsibility, self congruence, and self acceptance leads to more errors in multiple cognitive operations.
20. The Effortful Control (EC) of Students with and without Learning Disabilities shows a significant difference. That is, the Students with Learning Disabilities have low scores in the areas of attention, inhibitory control and activation control than compared to Students without Learning Disabilities.
21. There is a significant difference in Surgency (S) between the Students with and without Learning Disabilities. That is the Students with Learning Disabilities have low Surgency (S) factors like, high intensity pleasure, shy, and fear when compared to Students without Learning Disabilities.
22. There is a significant difference in temperament between Students with Learning Disabilities and without Learning Disabilities. It shows that the temperament scores of Students with Learning Disabilities lower than that of the Students without Learning Disabilities. Temperament variability has been described to neurophysiologic variations in brain functioning of Students with Learning Disabilities.
23. There is a significant difference between Self-Directedness (SD) of Students with Learning Disabilities and Students without Learning Disabilities. It shows that the goal directedness, fluency of ideas, and sense of responsibility, self congruence, and self acceptance are low in Students with Learning Disabilities than the Students without Learning Disabilities.
24. The scores of Cooperativeness (CO) among Students with and without Learning Disabilities have significant difference. Which means that the Students with Learning Disabilities have low in social acceptance, empathy, helpfulness, compassion for others, and conscience than Students without Learning Disabilities.
25. There is a significant difference in Self-Transcendence (ST) among Students with and without Learning Disabilities. That is, when compared to Students without Learning Disabilities, the Students with Learning Disabilities have low in Self-Transcendence (ST), which means that they are not much interested in spirituality.

26. The character between Students with Learning Disabilities and without Learning Disabilities shows a significant difference. That the Students with Learning Disabilities have low self directedness, cooperativeness and self transcendence of character dimensions than the Students without Learning Disabilities.
27. The correct responses of executive functions of Students with and without Learning Disabilities have significant difference. Since Students with Learning Disabilities are low scored that they have significant difficulty to recognize the significance of unexpected situations and to make alternative plans quickly when unusual events arise and interfere with normal routines.
28. There is a significant difference in the error responses of executive functions of students with and without Learning Disabilities. This means that the Students with Learning Disabilities have low level of planning and problem solving ability than Students without Learning Disabilities. They have the difficulty to follow rules, utilizing environmental feedback and goal directed behavior.
29. The perseverative responses of executive functions among Students with and without Learning Disabilities show a significant difference and therefore the Students with Learning Disabilities have more perseveration than the students without Learning Disabilities. Thus, their thinking appeared to be extremely perseverative, so they begin with an unsuccessful approach to a new problem or situation. They might continue with that unsuccessful approach, well beyond the point where others would seek alternative solutions.
30. There is a significant difference in perseverative error responses of the Students with and without Learning Disabilities. This means that Students with Learning Disabilities appeared to have difficulty with cognitive flexibility. Their thinking begins with an unsuccessful approach to a new problem or situation.
31. The conceptual level responses of Students with and without Learning Disabilities have a significant difference. It shows that the Students with Learning Disabilities are unable to retain new information and maintain recent information. The concept formation of Students with Learning Disabilities reflects the inefficient brain processing and patterning or impairment in the capacity to scan and select.
32. There is significant difference in Self-Transcendence (ST) between the age group of 13 to 14 and 15 to 16. That means the interest in spirituality and fantasy are more in the age group of 15 to 16 than with the age group of 13 to 14.
33. There is a significant difference in the character between the age group of 13 to 14 and 15 to 16. This shows that the character dimensions of

self directedness, cooperativeness and self transcendence are higher in the age group of 13 to 14 than the age group of 15 to 16.

34. There is more significant links between temperament and executive functions among Students with Learning Disabilities than that of Students without Learning Disabilities. It is evident that the significant relationships between temperament and executive functions among Students with Learning Disabilities and without Learning Disabilities, which means that the high genetic or biological traits are make more problems in executive functions of the Students with Learning Disabilities than that of Students without Learning Disabilities.
35. There is only a significant link between character and executive functions among Students with Learning Disabilities, whereas the Students without Learning Disabilities have no significant links between character and executive functions. It is evident that the Students with Learning Disabilities have low goal directedness, fluency of ideas, and sense of responsibility, self congruence, and self acceptance leads to more errors in multiple cognitive operations.

SUMMARY

The present study aimed to find out the temperament, character and executive functions among students with learning disabilities and without learning disabilities. The study has been carried out in two phases. In the first phase, the instrument, Early Adolescent Temperament Character Inventory (EATCI) was developed for assessing temperament and character of the participants. In the second phase, the EATCI and Wisconsin Card Sorting Test (WCST) were used to collect data. WCST is a well-established measure of executive function. The participants of the present study were 40 students with learning disabilities and 40 without learning disabilities. Descriptive research design was used for the present study. In order to find out the objectives and to test hypotheses, the statistical techniques such as; the comparison of mean, median, mode, skeweness, kurtosis and standard deviation, student 't' test and correlation were used for the present study. The findings of the study reveal that there is significant difference in temperament, character and executive functions among students with learning disabilities and without learning disabilities. The executive functions of students with learning disabilities had a significant moderate relationship with temperament [especially in the dimensions of Effortful Control (EC), Surgency (S) and Affiliativeness (AF)] and character [Self-Directedness (SD) only]. In the case of students without learning disabilities, the executive functions had a significant moderate relationship with temperament only.

Strengths of the Study

The study has the following strengths.

- **The new instrument:** in this study, the new instrument was developed for assessing temperament and character of early adolescents in Kerala. This unique attempt has got immense scope for the research in the field of educational settings, family, clinic settings and to the society.
- **Pioneer in the area:** the studyis the first reporting the temperament, character and executive functions among students with and without learning disabilities. Also it is a neuropsychological study. This may lead to the new enlightenment in the area of learning disabilities.
- **Response rate:** in this study the information directly collected from carefully selected sample of respondents to describe the characteristics of population. Face to face informal interview is got good responses.
- **Administering and scoring instrument:** the most difficult instrument of executive function was used in this present study. Manual scoring of the instrument WCST is one of the marking strength of the present study.

Weakness of the Study

The study has got a few limitations.

- The study only assess in the areas of strategic planning, organized searching, utilizing environmental feedback to shift cognitive sets, directing behavior toward achieving goal and modulating impulsive responding of executive functions.
- The selection of the sample was only taken from three districts of Kerala and also the sample size is reduced after screening tests.
- The study couldn't approach the intervention methods of the areas of the title.

IMPLICATIONS

The present study is a unique work focused on neuro-physical and neuro-psychological aspects in the field of learning disabilities. The study found that, there is more links between temperament and executive functions among Students with Learning Disabilities than that of Students without Learning Disabilities. The temperament was low in Students with Learning Disabilities, whereas the character was high in Students without Learning Disabilities. The Students with Learning Disabilities have more association betweentemperament with executive functions than the character. The study also reveals the Students without Learning Disabilities have a link between temperament and executive functions than with the character. The Students with Learning Disabilities has difficulties in regulates goal-directed behaviour. Therefore, in one word, the study explains that temperament and character are influence the cognitive skills of the Students with and without Learning Disabilities also. The findings of the research have implementation and evaluation of specific intervention focusing on the issues of Students with Learning Disabilities. This is efforts directed teachers, parents and specialists for the awareness of the problems of behaviour in the students with learning disabilities

SUGGESSIONS FOR FURTHER RESEARCH

This research found a moderate significant relationship between temperament, character and executive functions, which gives inspiration to further research.The present study confronted certain clarifications which will be suggested for the new discoveries in the field of related areas.

1. The same study can be conducted with the help of new advanced psychological tools and techniques to understand the personality aspects and the cognitive domains of the Students with Learning Disabilities.
2. Further studies can be conducted to include in the sub domains of temperament also.
3. The intervention methods are also suggested for further research which will be needful for the problems of Students with Learning Disabilities.
4. To include the parental inventory to the self report of EATCI for further research, it leads more accuracy in the temperament and character.

CONCLUSION

Temperament is biologically based: Heredity, neural, and hormonal factors affect response to the environment where as the character is weakly heritable and are influenced by learning and the family environment. Executive functions describe a set of cognitive abilities that control and regulate other abilities and behaviours. These are necessary for goal-directed behaviour. They include the ability to initiate and stop actions, to monitor and change behaviour as needed, and to plan future behaviour when faced with novel tasks and situations. Executive functions allow us to anticipate outcomes and adapt to changing situations. The ability to form concepts and think abstractly is often considered components of executive function.

The present study was intended to explore the temperament, character and executive functions among Students with Learning Disabilities and without Learning Disabilities. From the study, the results indicate that there is more links between temperament and executive functions among Students with Learning Disabilities than Students without Learning Disabilities. It reveals that, except Negative Affect (NA), the other domains of temperament such as Effortful Control (EC), Surgency (S) and Affiliativeness (AF) are linked to the executive functions. The result reveals that there is links between characterand total number of errors of executive functions among Students with Learning Disabilities. That is the environmental interactions and the

Self Directedness (SD) such as, goal directedness, fluency of ideas, and sense of responsibility, self congruence, and self acceptanceare adversely affecting their inherited cognitive issues. In the case of Students without Learning Disabilities, they only have morelinks between Effortful Control (EC) of temperament and executive functions; the character was less affected in their execution of brain.Also there is a difference in Effortful Control (EC) and Surgency (S) of temperament scores among Students with and without Learning Disabilities. That is, the genetic variations were present in the Students with Learning Disabilities, which explain that the Students with Learning Disabilities have lowin the areas of attention, inhibitory control, activation control,sensation seeking or high intensity pleasure, shyness and fear. These variations are creating more problems in their neurological functions of the brain.

Most of the Students without Learning Disabilities shows that the average or above average performance of the Wisconsin Card Sorting Test (WCST) where as the scores of the Students with Learning Disabilities shows impairment in their strategic planning, organized searching, utilizing environmental feedback to shift cognitive sets, directing behaviour toward achieving a goal, and modulating impulsive responding. The perseverative responses are more in Students with Learning Disabilities where as the conceptual level responses are high in Students without Learning Disabilities. This means that the capacity of the Students with Learning Disabilities engage in logical analysis was impaired than the Students without Learning Disabilities. They appeared to have difficulty with cognitive flexibility. Their thinking appeared to be extremely perseverative, and should they begin with an unsuccessful approach to a new problem or situation. They might well continue with that unsuccessful approach well beyond the point where others would seek alternative solutions. The Students without Learning Disabilities are maintaining correct sorting principle of the Wisconsin Card Sorting Test (WCST) and, they are able to retain new information and maintain recent information.

The age group of 13 to 14 years have high in character (especially in the dimension of Self-Transcendence) than with the age group of 15 to 16. That is, they have more spirituality and fantasy. The study explains that the other aspects of temperament and executive functions are not shows any differences in the age group.

Over all, the results of the study reveals that the Students with Learning Disabilities have more link between inherited traits (temperament) with set of cognitive abilities that are control and regulate behaviours (executive functions) than the individual differences in self concepts about goals and values (character).The Students without Learning Disabilities has also a link between temperament and certain areas of executive functions than with character. When compared to Students with and without Learning Disabilities, the inherited traits are low in Students with Learning Disabilities, whereas the individual differences in self concepts about goals and values are high in Students without Learning Disabilities. The Students with Learning Disabilities has difficulties in regulates goal-directed behaviour. That is, they have problems in the ability to initiate and stop activities, to monitor and change behaviour as required, and to plan future behavior when faced with novel tasks and situations.

References

Alarco'n, M., Knopik, V.S., & DeFries, J.C. (2000). Co-variation of Mathematics Achievement and General Cognitive Ability in Twins. *Journal of School Psychology*, 38, 63-77.

Allport, G.W. (1937). *Personality: A Psychological Interpretation*. New York: Holt Press.

Allport, G.W., & Odbert, H.S. (1936). Trait Names: A Psycho-lexical Study. *Psychological Monographs*, 47 (211).

Alverez, J.A., & Emory, E. (2006). Executive Functioning and the Frontal Lobes: A Meta-analytic Review. *Neuropsychology Review*, 16, 17-42.

American Psychiatric Association (2013). Diagnostic and Statistical Manual for Mental Disorders-5TM. *American Psychiatric Publishing*. Washington, DC London, England.

Anckarsater, H., Stahlberg, O., Larson, T., Hakansson, C., Jutblad, S.B., Niklasson, L., & Rastam, M. (2006). The Impact of ADHD and Autism Spectrum Disorders on Temperament, Character, and Personality Development. *American Journal of Psychiatry*, 163, 1239-1244.

Anderson, J.R., Reder, L.M., & Simon, H.A. (1995). Applications and Misapplications of Cognitive Psychology to Mathematics Education. Unpublished Paper, Carnegie Mellon University, Department of Psychology, Pittsburgh. Available from http://act.psy.cmu.edu/personal/ ja/misapplied.html.

Anderson, S.W., Damasio, H., Jones, R.D., & Tranel, D. (1991). Wisconsin Card Sorting Test Performance as a measure of Frontal Lobe Damage. *Journal of Clinical and Experimental Neuropsychology*, 13, 909-922.

Anderson, S.W. (2002). Assessment and Development of Executive Functions during Childhood. *Child Neuropsychology*. 8, 71-82.

Andres, P. (2003). Frontal Cortex as the Central Executive of Working Memory: Time to Revise our View. *Cortex*, 39, 871-895.

Anu, G. (2016). A Study on the Quality of Life of Children with Cerebral Palsy: Unpublished Doctoral Thesis. Faculty of Behavioural Sciences. Mahatma Gandhi University. Kerala.

Aram, D.M., Gillespie, L.L., & Yamashita, T.S. (1990). Reading among Children with Left and Right Brain Lesions. *Developmental Neuropsychology,* 6(4), 301-317.

Aram, D.M., & Ekelman, B.L. (1988). Scholastic Aptitude and Achievement among Children with Unilateral Brain Lesions. *Neuropsychologia,* 26 (6), 903-916. 1976, Cited in DeFries, 1991)

Ardila, A., & Surloff, C. (2004). Dysexecutive Syndromes. *Medlink Neurology.* San Diego: Arbor Publishing Co. Ashcraft, M.H., Yamashita, T.S., & Aram, D.M. (1992). Mathematics Performance in Left and Right Brain-lesioned Children and Adolescents. *Brain and Cognition,* 19, 208-252.

Association for Children with Learning Disabilities. (1986, September-October). ACLD Description: Specific Learning Disabilities. *ACLD Newbriefs,* 15-16.

Axelrod., Robert., Robert, A., Joshua, E, & Cohen, M.D. (1996). Aligning Simulation Models: *A Case Study and Results, Computational and Mathematical Organization Theory* 1, 123-141.

Baddeley, A. (1986). *Working Memory.* Oxford: Oxford University Press.

Baddeley, A. (1998). The Central Executive: A Concept and Some Misconceptions. *Journal of the International Neuropsychological Society,* 4, 523-526.

Baddeley, A. (2002). Fractionating the Central Executive. In D.T. Stuss & R.T. Knight (Eds.), *Principles of Frontal Lobe Function.* New York: Oxford University Press Inc.

Baddeley, A.D. (1992). Working Memory. *Science,* 225, 556-559.

Baddeley, A.D., & Hitch, G.J. (1974). Working Memory. In The Psychology of Learning and Motivation, Vol. 8, ed. G.A. Bower. New York: *Academic Press*, pp. 47-89.

Baddeley, A., & Logie, R. (1999). Working Memory: The Multiple Component Model. In A. Miyake, & P. Shah (Eds.) *Models of Working Memory: Mechanisms of Active Maintenance and Executive Control* (pp. 28-61). New York: Cambridge University Press.

Baddeley, A., & Wilson, B. (1988). Frontal Amnesia and the Dysexecutive Syndrome. *Brain and Cognition,* 7, 212-230.

Bakker, (1992). Neuropsychological Classification and Treatment of Dyslexia. *Journal of Learning Disabilities,* 25 (2), 102-109.

Bakwin, H. (1973). Reading Disability in Twins. *Developmental Medicine and Child Neurology,* 15(2), 184-187.

Barceló, F. (1999). Electrophysiological Evidence of Two Different Types of Error in the Wisconsin Card Sorting Test. *Neuroreport,* 10, 1299-1303.

Barceló, F. (2001). Does the Wisconsin Card Sorting Test measure Prefrontal Function? The Spanish Journal of Psychology, 4, 79-100.

Barceló, F., & Knight, R.T. (2002). Both Random and Perseverative Errors Underlie WCST Deficits in Prefrontal Patients. *Neuropsychologia,* 40, 349-356.

Barceló, F., Escera, C., Corral, M.J., & Periañez, J.A. (2006). Task Switching and Novelty Processing Activate a Common Neural Network for Cognitive Control. *Journal of Cognitive Neuroscience,* 18, 1734-1748.

Been, P.H. (1994). Dyslexia and Irregular Dynamics of the Visual System. In K.P. Van Den Bos, L.S. Siegel, D.J. Bakker, & D.L. Share (Eds.), *Current Directions in Dyslexia Research* (pp. 93-116). Lisse, The Netherlands: Swets & Zeitlinger.

Bender, L. (1957). Specific Reading Disability as Maturational Lag. *Bulletin of the Orton Society,*7, 9-18.

Bender, L.A. (1956). *Psychology of Children with Organic Brain Disorders.* Springer Field, IL: Charles. C. Thomas.

Bender, L.A. (1957). Specific Reading Disability as a Maturational Lag. *Bulletin of the Orton Society,* 7, 9-18.

Benton, A.L. (1975). Developmental Dyslexia: Neuropsychological Aspects. In W.J. Fried Lander: *Advances in Neurology* (Vol. 7, pp. 1-47). New York: Raven Press.

Berg, E.A. (1948). A Simple Objective Test for Measuring Flexibility Thinking. *Journal of General Psychology,* 39, 15-22.

Bergvall, A.H., Nilsson, T., & Hansen, S. (2003). Exploring the Link between Character, Personality Disorder and Neuropsychological Function. *European Psychiatry,* 18, 334-344.

Berk, L.E. (1992). Children's Private Speech: An Overview of Theory and the States of Research. In R.M. Diaz & L.E. Berk (Eds.), Private Speech form Social Interaction to Self Regulation. Hillsdale, N.J. Erlbaum.

Berkow, R., & Fletcher, A.J. (1992). *The Merck Manual of Diagnosis and Therapy.* (16th Ed). Rahway. NJ: Merck research laboratories. 2844 pp. https://doi.org/10.1016/S0001-2092(07)68455-5

Berman, K.F., Ostrem, J.L., Randolph, C., Gold, J., Goldberg, T.E., & Coppola, R., *et al.* (1995). Physiological Activation of a Cortical Network during Performance of the Wisconsin Card Sorting Test: A Positron Emission Tomography Study. *Neuropsychologia,* 33, 1027-1046.

Bigler, E.D. (1992). The Neurobiology and Neuropsychology of Adult Learning Disorders. Journal of Learning Disabilities, 25, 488-506.

Birch, H.G., & Belmont, L. (1965). Lateral Dominance, Lateral Awareness and Reading Disability. *Child Development,* 36, 57-71.

Blakemore, S.J., & Choudhury, S. (2006). Development of the Adolescent Brain: Implications for Executive Function and Social Cognition. *J Child Psychol Psychiatry.* 47(3-4): 296-312.https://doi.org/10.1111/j.1469-7610.2006.01611.x

Blank, M., & Bridger, W.H. (1966). Cross Model Transfer in Nursery School Children. Journal of Comparative & Physiological Psychology, 58, 227-282.

Boeker, H., Klieser, M., Lehman, D., Jaenke, L., Bogerts, B., & Northoff, G. (2006). Executive Dysfunction, Self and Ego Pathology in Schizophrenia: An Exploratory Study of Neuropsychology and Personality. *Comprehensive Psychiatry,* 47, 7-19.

Bohman M., Cloninger, C.R., Sigvardsson, S., & Von Knorring, A.L. (1982). Predisposition to petty Criminality in Swedish Adoptees. I. Genetic and Environmental Heterogeneity. *Archives of General Psychiatry,* 39, 1233-1241.

Bohman, M., Cloninger, C.R., von Knorring, A.L., & Sigvardsson, S. (1984). An Adoption Study of Somatoform Disorders. III. Cross-fostering Analysis and Genetic Relationship to Alcoholism and Criminality. *Archives of General Psychiatry,* 41, 872-878.

Bohman, M., Sigvardsson, S., & Cloninger, C.R. (1981). Maternal Inheritance of Alcohol Abuse. Cross-fostering Analysis of Adopted Women. *Archives of General Psychiatry,* 38, 965-969.

Bond, A.J. (2001). Neurotransmitters, Temperament and Social Functioning. *European Neuro Psycho Pharmacology,* 11, 261-274. Retrieved from http://www.innopac.up.ac.za

Border, E. (1971). Developmental Dyslexia Prevailing Diagnostic Approach. In Myklebust, H. R. (Ed.), *Progress on Learning Disabilities,* 3, 85-121, New York, Grune and Stratton.

Branch, W.B., Cohen, M.J., & Hynd, G.W. (1995). Academic Achievement and Attention-deficit/hyperactivity Disorder in Children with Left- or Right Hemisphere Dysfunction. *Journal of Learning Disabilities,* 28(1), 35-43, 64.

Brändström, S. (2009). Personality and its Complexity; An Investigation of the Swedish version of the Temperament and Character Inventory. *Sweden. Department of Clinical and Experimental Medicine, Psychiatry Section, Linköping University.*

Bryant, P., & Bradley, L. (1980). Why Children Sometimes Write Words which they do not Read. In Frith, U., Cognitive Processes in Spelling. London: Academic Press.

Bryant, P., & Bradley, L. (1983). Psychological Strategies in the Development of Reading and Writing. In Martlew, M., The Psychology of Written Language. Chichester: JHN Wiley.

Byrne, B., Wadsworth, S., Corley, R., Samuelsson, S., Quain, P., DeFries, J.C., Willcutt, E., & Olson, R.K. (2005). Longitudinal Twin Study of Early Literacy Development: Preschool and Kindergarten Phases. *Scientific Studies of Reading*, 9, 219-235.

Cardon, L.R., Smith, S.D., Fulker, D.W., Kimberling, W.J., Pennington, B.F., & DeFries, J.C. (1994). Quantitative Trait Locus for Reading Disability in Chromosome 6. *Science*, 266, 276-279.

Carlson, M.S. (2015). Executive Functions in Context: Development, Measurement, Theory an Experience. *JSTORonlinepublications*. 138-151.

Cassimjee, N., & Murphy, R. (2010) Studied Temperament and Character Correlates of Neuropsychological Performance South African Journal of Psychology, 40(2), 2010, pp. 125-138.

Catafau, A.M., Parellada, E., Lomena, F.J., Bernardo, M., Pavia, J., & Ros, D., *et al.* (1994). Prefrontal and Temporal Blood Flow in Schizophrenia: Resting and Activation Technetium-99m-HMPAO SPECT Patterns in Young Neuroleptic Naive Patients with Acute Disease. *The Journal of Nuclear Medicine*, 35, 935-941.

Catafau, A., Parellada, E., Lomena, F., Bernardo, M., Setoain, J., & Catarineu, S. (1998). Role of the Cingulate Gyrus during the Wisconsin Card Sorting Test: A Single Photon Emission Computed Tomography Study in Normal Volunteers. *Psychiatry Research: Neuroimaging*, 26, 67-74.

Cattell, R.B. (1943). The Description of Personality: Basic Traits Resolved into Clusters. *The Journal of Abnormal and Social Psychology*, 38(4), 476-506.

Chase, C.H. (1996). A Visual Deficit Model of Developmental Dyslexia. In C.H. Chase, G.D. Rosen, & G.F. Sherman (Eds.), *Developmental dyslexia: Neural, Cognitive, and Genetic Mechanisms* (pp. 127-156). Baltimore, MD: York Press.

Chase, C., & Jenner, A.R. (1993). Magnocellular Visual Deficits Affect Temporal Processing of Dyslexics. *Annals of the New York Academy of Sciences*, 682, 326-329.

Chelune, G.J., & Baer, R.L. (1986). Developmental Norms for the Wisconsin Card Sorting Test. *Journal of Clinical and Experimental Neuro psychology*, 8, 219-228.

Cho, S.C., Jung, S.W., Kim, B.N., Hwang, J.W., Shin, M.S., Kim, J.W., & Kim, H.W. (2009). Temperament and Character among Korean Children and Adolescents with Anxiety Disorders. *European Child & Adolescent Psychiatry*, 18, 60-64.

Christensen, N.I. (1996) Poisson's Ratio and Crustal Seismology. Journal of Geophysical Research, 101, 3139-3156. http://dx.doi.org/10.1029/95JB 03446

Cicek, M., & Nalcaci, E. (2001). Inter Hemispheric Asymmetry of EEG Alpha Activity at Rest and during the Wisconsin Card Sorting Test: Relations with Performance. *Biological Psychology,* 58, 75-88.

Clair-Thompson, H.L., & Gathercole, S.E. (2006). Executive Functions and Achievements in School: Shifting, Updating, Inhibition and Working Memory. SAGE Journals, 59, http://journals.sagepub.com/doi/10.1080/17470210 500162854

Clements, S.D. (1996). *Minimal Brain Dysfunction in Children* (NINDS Monograph No. 3, U.S. Public Health Service Publication No. 1415). Washington, DC: U.S. Government Printing Office.

Cloninger C.R. (2004), *Feeling Good: The Science of Well Being*. New York: Oxford University Press.

Cloninger, C.R, Sigvardsson S, Von Knorring A.L., & Bohman M. (1984). An Adoption Study of Somatoform Disorders. II. Identification of Two Discrete Somatoform Disorders. *Archives of General Psychiatry,* 41, 863-871.

Cloninger, C.R. (1987). A Systematic method for Clinical Description and Classification of Personality Variants. *Archives of General Psychiatry,* 44, 573-588.

Cloninger, C.R., & Svrakic, N.M. (1997). Integrative Psychobiological Approach to Psychiatric Assessment and Treatment. *Psychiatry,* 60, 120-141. Retrieved from http://www.innopac.up.ac.za

Cloninger, C.R., Bohman, M., & Sigvardsson, S. (1981). Inheritance of Alcohol Abuse. Cross Fostering Analysis of Adopted Men. *Archives of General Psychiatry,* 38, 861-868.

Cloninger, C.R., Przybeck, T.R., Svrakic, D.M., & Wetzel, R.D. (1994). The Temperament and Character Inventory: A Guide to its Development and Use, Center for Psychobiology of Personality, St. Louis.

Cloninger, C.R., Sigvardsson S., Bohman M., &, Von Knorring, A.L. (1982). Predisposition to Petty Criminality in Swedish Adoptees. II. Cross-fostering Analysis of Gene-environment Interaction. *Archives of General Psychiatry,* 39, 1242-1247.

Cloninger, C.R., Svrakic, D.M., & Przybeck, T.R. (1993). A Psychobiological Model of Temperament and Character. *Archives of General Psychiatry,* 50(12), 975- 990. doi:10.1001/archpsyc.1993.01820240059008

Cloninger, S. (2000). *Theories of Personality: Understanding Persons. (3rd edition).* Upper Saddle River, HJ: Prentice-Hall, Inc.

Coelho, V.M. *et al.,* (2012). P-565-Catechol-o-methyltransferase Activity in Erythrocytes from Patients with Eating Disorders. *European Psychiatry,* 27, p. 1. Available at: http://dx.doi.org/10.1016/S0924-9338(12)74732-6

Cohen, M., Town, P., & Buff, A. (1988). Neuro Developmental Differences in Confrontational Naming in Children. *Developmental Neuropsychology*, 4, 75-81.

Collette, T., & Van der Linden, M. (2002). Brain Imaging of the Central Executive Component of Working Memory. *Neuroscience and Biobehavior Review*, 26, 105-125.

Collette, T., Van der Linden, M., Laureys, S., Delfiore, G., Degueldre, C., & Luxen, A. (2005). Exploring the Unity and Diversity of the Neural Substrates of Executive Functioning. *Human Brain Mapping*, 25, 409-423.

Condor, A., Anderson, V., & Sailing, M. (1995). Do Reading Disabled Children have Planning Problems? *Developmental Neuropsychology*, 11(4), 485-502.

Conway, A., & Stifter, C.A. (2012). Longitudinal Antecedents of Executive Function in Preschoolers. *NHS Public Access*. Child Dev. Author Manuscript; Available in PMC 2013 May 1. Published in Final Edited form as: Child Dev. 2012 May; 83(3):1022-1036. Published online 2012 Mar 30. doi: 10.1111/j. 1467-8624.2012.01756.x

Cook. L., Don, D., Fuchs, D., Fletcher, M.J., & Frank, G. *et al*. Researcher Consensus Statement. [Online]. 2001 [cited 2006 Sept]; Available from: URL: http://www.nrcld.org/publications/digests/digest3.shtml

Corballis, M.C., & Beale, I.L. (1983). The Ambivalent Mind: The Neuro Psychology of Left & Right. Chicago: Nelson- Hall.

Corbetta, M., & Shulman, G.L. (2002). Control of Goal Directed and Stimulus Driven Attention in the Brain. *Nat Rev Neuroscience* 3: 201-15.

Corcoran, R., & Upton, D. (1993). A Role for the Hippocampus in Card Sorting? *Cortex*, 29, 293-304.

Cossu, G., Daprati, E., & Marshall, J.C. (1995). Deep Dyslexia and Right Hemisphere Hypothesis: Spoken and Written Language after Extensive Left Hemisphere Lesion in a 12 Year Old Boy. *Cognitive Neuropsychology*, 12 (4), 391-407.

Costa, P.T., & McCrae, R.R. (1995). Domains and Facets: Hierarchical Personality Assessment using the Revised NEO Personality Inventory. Journal of Personality Assessment, 64, 21-50.

Critchly, F. (1983). Ziggurats and Dendrograms. *University of Warwick Statistics. Research report*, 43.

Curley, J.F., & Ginard, R.J. (1990). A Computerized Visual-search Task as a Measure of Cerebral Dysfunction and Organization. *Perceptual and Motor Skills*, 71, 895-904.

Curtiss, S., & Tallal, P. (1988). Neuro Linguistic Correlates of Specific Developmental Language Impairment (Abstract). *Journal of Clinical of Clinical and Experimental Neuropsychology*, 10, 18-19.

D'Esposito, M., Postle, B., Ballard, D., & Lease, J. (1999). Maintenance versus Manipulation of Information held in Working Memory: An Event-related fMRI Study. *Brain and Cognition,* 41, 66-86.

Dawson, G., & Fischer, K.W. (Eds.). (1994). Human Behavior and the Developing Brain. New York: Guilford Press.

De Frias, C., Dixon, R., & Strauss, E. (2006). Structure of Tour Executive Functioning Tests in Healthy Older Adults. *Neuro Psychology,* 20, 206-214.

DeFries, J.C., Gillis, J.J., & Wadsworth, S.J. (1993). Genes and Genders: A Twin Study of Reading Disability. In A.M. Galaburda (Ed.), *Dyslexia and Development: Neurobiological Aspects of Extra-ordinary Brains* (pp. 187-203). London: Harvard University Press.

Delis, D.C., Squire, L.R., Bihrle, A., & Massman, P. (1992). Componential Analysis of Problem-solving Ability: Performance of Patients with Frontal Lobe Damage and Amnesic Patients on a New Sorting Test. *Neuropsychologia,* 30, 683-697.

Demakis, G.J. (2003). A Meta-analytic Review of the Sensitivity of the Wisconsin Card Sorting Test to Frontal and Lateralized Frontal Brain Damage. *Neuropsychology,* 17, 255-264.

Denckla, M. B. (2003). *Executive Functions.* Paper Presented at the Capital Area IDA Meeting, Washington, DC.

Dennison, L.K. (2012). The Relationship between Temperament, Character and Executive Functioning: (A Mini Dissertation Submitted in Partial Fulfilment of the Requirements for the Degree of Master of Arts in Counselling Psychology). Faculty of Humanities. *University of Pretoria.*

Devi, G.M.S., & Mustafa, K.M. (2018). Set Shifting Ability of Frontal Lobe Executive Functions among Students with Learning Disabilities and without Learning Disabilities. *International Multidisciplinary Journal of Cognitive Discourses* 5, (4) 2-13 Retrieved from: http://cdimj.nas publishers. com

DiLalla, L.F., & Jones, S. (2000). Genetic and Environmental Influences on Temperament in Preschoolers. In D.L. Molfese & V.J. Molfese (Eds.), Temperament and Personality Development Across the Life Span (pp. 33-55). Mahwah, NJ: Erlbaum.

Doehring, D.G., & Hoshko, I.M. (1977). Classification of Reading Problems by the Q-technique of Factor Analysis. *Cortex,* 13, 281-294.

Doehring, D.G., (1978). The Tangled Web of Behavioral Research on Developmental Dyslexia. In A.L. Benton & D. Pearl (Eds.), *Dyslexia: An Appraisal of Current Knowledge* (pp. 123-135). New York: Oxford University Press.

Doehring, D.G., Trites, R.L., Patel, P., & Fiedorowicz, C. (1981). *Reading Disabilities: The Interaction of Reading, Language and Neuropsychological Deficits.* New York: Academic Press.

Doidge, N. (2007). *The Brain that Changes itself: Stories of Personal Triumph from the Frontiers of Brain Science*. New York: Viking.

Doris, J. (1986). Learning Disabilities. In S.J. Ceci (Ed), *Handbook of Cognitive, Social, and Neuropsychological Aspects of Learning Disabilities* (Vol. I, pp. 3-53). Hillsdale, NJ: Erlbaum.

Drechsler, R., Logoz, M.Z., Walitzal, S., & Steinhausen, H.S. (2015). The Relations between Temperament, Character, and Executive Functions in Children with ADHD and Clinical Controls. *Journal of Attention Disorders* 1-12. sagepub.com/journalsPermissions.nav DOI:10.1177/1087054715583356.

Drewe, E.A. (1974). *The Effect of Type and Area of Brain Lesion on Wisconsin Card Sorting Test Performance.* Cortex, 10, 159-170.

Duncan, J., Emslie, H., Williams, P., Johnson, R., & Freer, C. (1996). Intelligence and the Frontal Lobes: The Organization of Goal Directed Behavior. *Cognitive Psychology,* 30, 257-303.

Eden, G.F., Stein, J.F., Wood, H.M., & Wood, F.B. (1995a). Temporal and Spatial Processing in Reading Disabled and Normal Children. *Cortex,* 31, 451-468.

Eden, G.F., Stein, J.F., Wood, H.M., & Wood, F.B. (1995b). Verbal and Visual Problems in Reading Disability. *Journal of Learning Disabilities,* 28(5), 272-290.

Eden, G.F., Stein, J.F., Wood, M.H., & Wood, F.B. (1993). Dyslexia: A Study of Preserved and Impaired Visuospatial and Phonological Functions. *Annals of the New York Academy of Sciences,* 682, 335-338.

Eden, G.F., Van Meter, J.W., Rumsey, J.M., Maisog, J.M., Woods, R.P., & Zeffiro, T.A. (1996). Abnormal Processing of Visual Motion in Dyslexia Revealed by Functional Brain Imaging. *Brain,* 382, 66-69.

Eldreth, D.A., Patterson, M.D., Porcelli, A.J., Biswal, B.B., Rebbechi, D., & Rypma, B. (2006). Evidence for Multiple Manipulation Processes in Prefrontal Cortex. *Brain Research.* 1123: 145-156.

Eling, P., Derckx, K., & Maes, R. (2008). On the Historical and Conceptual Background of the Wisconsin Card Sorting Test. *Brain and Cognition,* 67, 247-253.

Eysenck, H.J. (1999). *Dimensions of Personality*. Florence, KY: Routledge.

Faraone, S.V., Kunwar, A., Adamson, J., & Biederman, J. (2009). Personality Traits among ADHD Adults: Implications of Late-onset and sub Threshold Diagnoses. *Psychological Medicine* 39(4): 685-93.

Fawcett, A.J., Nicolson, R.I., & Dean, P. (1996). Impaired Performance of Children with Dyslexia on a Range of Cerebellar Tasks. *Annals of Dyslexia,* 46, 259-283.

Fiedorowicz, C. (1986). Training of Component Reading Skills. *Annals of Dyslexia,* 36, 318-334.

Fiedorowicz, C., & Trites, R.L. (1991). From Theory to Practice with Subtypes of Reading Disabilities. In B.P. Rourke (Ed.), *Neuropsychological Validation of Learning Disability Subtypes.* New York: Guilford Press.

Field, A. (2012). *Discovering Statistics using IBM SPSS Statistics* (4th ed). New Delhi: SAGE Publications India Pvt. Ltd.

Finucci, J., Guthrie, J., Childs, A., Abbey, H., & Childs, B. (1976). The Genetics of Specific Reading Disability. *Annals of Human Genetics,* 40: 1-23.

Fisher, J.H. (1905). Gase of Congenital Word Blindness (Inability to Learn to Read). *Ophthdmological Review,* 24, 315.

Flowers, D.L., Wood, F.B., & Nailer, C.E. (1991). A Regional Cerebral Blood Flow Correlates of Language Processes in Reading Disability. *Achieves of Neurology,* 48, 637-643.

Freedman, M., Black, S., Ebert, P., & Binns, M. (1998). Orbitofrontal Function, Object Alternation and Perseveration. *Cerebral Cortex,* 8, 18-27.

Fritch, D., Friston, K.J., Liddle, P.F., & Frackowiak, R.S.J. (1991). A PET Study of Word Finding. *Neuropsychologia,* 29, 1137-1148.

Frith, U. (1980). *Cognitive Processes in Spelling*. London: Academic Press.

Frosting, M. (1964). Frosting Developmental Test of Visual Perception. *Palo Alto, C.A: Consulting Psychologists Press.*

Fuller & Thompson (1978). *Foundations of Behaviour Genetics.* Saint Louis : Mosby.

Gaddes, W.H. (1985). Learning Disabilities and Brain Function: A Neuro Psychological Approach (2nd edn). New York: Springer – verlag.

Gay, L.R. (1990). Educational Research: Competencies for Analysis and Application (3rd Ed.). New York: Merrill Publishing Co.

Geary, D.C. (2003). Learning Disabilities and Arithmetic: Problem Solving Differences and Cognitive Deficits. In H.L. Swanson, K.R. Harris, & S. Graham (Eds.), *Handbook of Learning Disabilities.* NewYork, NY: Guilford.

Gerstmann, J. (1924). Fingeragnosie: eine umschriebene Stbrung der Orientierung am Eigenen Korper. *Wien Klin Wochenechr,* 37, 1010-1012.

Geschwind, N. (1964). The Development of the Brain and the Evolution of Language. *Monograph Series on Language & Linguistics,* 17, 155-169.

Geschwind, N., & Behan, P. (1982). Left-handedness: Association with Immune Disease, Migraine, and Developmental Learning Disorder. *Proceedings of the National Academy of Sciences of the U S A.*

Gillespie, N.A., Cloninger, C.R., Heath, A.C., & Martin, N.G. (2003). The Genetic Environmental Relationship between Cloninger's Dimensions of Temperament and Character. *Personality and Individual Differences,* 35, 1931-1946. doi:10.1016/S0191-8869(03)00042-4

Ginsburg, H.P. (1997). Mathematics Learning Disabilities. A View from Developmental Psychology. Journal of Learning Disabilities, 30, 20-33.

Giovagnoli, A.R. (2001). Relation of Sorting Impairment to Hippocampal Damage in Temporal Lobe Epilepsy. *Neuropsychological;* 39: 140-50.

Glass, G.V., & Hopkins, K.D. (1984). *Statistical Methods in Education and Psychology (2nd Ed.).* Englewood Cliffs, N.J.: Prentice-Hall.

Gliem, R., & Gliem, J. (2003). Calculating, Interpreting and Reporting Cronbach's Alpha Reliability Coefficient for Likert Type Scales. Retrieved from https://scholarworks.Iupui.edu/handle 1805/344.

Gnys, J.A., & Willis, W.G.(1991). Validation of Executive Function Tasks with Young Children. *Developmental Neuropsychology,* 7, 487-501.

Golberg, E. (2001). *The Executive Brain: Frontal Lobes and the Civilized Mind.* New York: Oxford University Press.

Goldberg, L.R. (1981). Language and Individual Differences: The Search for Universals in Personality Lexicons. In L.Wheeler (Ed.), Review of Personality and Social Psychology, (Vol. 2, pp. 141-165). Beverly Hills, CA: Sage.

Goldberg, T.E., Weinberger, D.R., Berman, K.F., Pliskin, N.H., & Podd, M.H. (1987). Further Evidence for Dementia of the Prefrontal Type in Schizophrenia? A Controlled Study of Teaching the Wisconsin Card Sorting Test. *Archives of General Psychiatry,* 44, 1008-1014.

Goldstein, B., Obrzut, J.E., John, C., Ledakis, G., & Armstrong, C. L. (2004). The Impact of Frontal and Non-frontal Brain Tumor Lesions on Wisconsin Card Sorting Test Performance. *Brain and Cognition,* 54, 110-116.

Gonzalez-Hernandez, J.A., Cedeno, I., Pita-Alcorta, C., Galan, L., Aubert, E., & Figueredo-Rodriguez, P. (2003). Induced Oscillations and the Distributed Cortical Sources during the Wisconsin Card Sorting Test Performance in Schizophrenic Patients: New Clues to Neural Connectivity. *International Journal of Psychophysiology,* 48, 11-24.

Gonzalez-Hernandez, J.A., Pita-Alcorta, C., Cedeno, I., Bosch-Bayard, J., Galan-Garcia, L., Scherbaum, W.A., *et al.* (2002). Wisconsin Card Sorting Test Synchronizes the Prefrontal, Temporal and Posterior Association Cortex in Different Frequency Ranges and Extensions. *Human Brain Mapping,* 17, 37-47.

Graczyk, P.A., Weissberg, R.P., Payton, J.W., Elias, M.J., Greenberg, M.T., & Zins, J.P. (2000). A Framework for Evaluating School-based Programs that Promote Social and Emotional Learning. In R. Bar-On & J.D.A. Parker (Eds.), *The Handbook of Emotional Intelligence.* San Francisco: Jossey-Bass.

Grant, D.A., & Berg, E.A. (1948). A Behavioural Analysis of Degree of Reinforcement and Ease of Shifting Response in a Weigl-type Card Sorting Problem. *Journal of Experimental Psychology,* 34, 404-411.

Green, M.F., Satz, P., Ganzell, S., & Vaclav, J.F. (1992).Wisconsin Card Sorting Test Performance in Schizophrenia: Remediation of a Stubborn Deficit. *American Journal of Psychiatry*, 149, 62-67.

Greenstone, H. (2011). Executive Function in the Classroom: Neurological Implications for Classroom Intervention. *Learning Landscapes*, 5(1),101-114.

Grewel, F. (1969). The Acalculias, in Disorders of Speech Perception and Symbolic Behaviour (eds P.J. Vinken & G.W. Bruyn). *Amsterdam: North-Holland publishing Company*, 4, pp. 187-194.

Hallahan, D.P., & Mercer, C.D. (2001). *Learning Disabilities: Historical Perspectives*. Washington, DC: Office of Special Education Programs, U.S. Department of Education.

Hallgren, B. (1950). Specific dyslexia (Congenital Word Blindness): A Clinical and Genetic Study. *Acta Psychiatrica et Neurologica Supplement*, 65, 1-287.

Hammill, D.D. (1993). A Timely Definition of Learning Disabilities: *Family and Community Health*, 16(3), 1-8.

Hammill, D.D., & Larsen, S.C. (1974). The Effectiveness of Psycholinguistic Training. Exceptional Children, 41, 5-15.

Hammill, D.D., Leigh, J.E., McNutt, G., & Larsen, S.C. (1981). A New Definition of Learning Disabilities. *Learning Disabilities Quarterly*, 4, 336-342.

Heaton, R.K. (1981). The Wisconsin Card Sorting Test Manual. *Odessa: Psychological Assessment Resources Inc.*

Heaton, R.K., Chelune, G.J., Talley, J.L., Kay, G.G., & Curtis, G. (1993). *Wisconsin Card Sorting Test (WCST). Manual Revised and Expanded*. Odessa, FL: Psychological Assessment Resources.

Heaton, S.K., Chelune, G.J., Talley, J.L., Kay, G.G., & Curtiss, G. (1993). Wisconsin Card Sorting Test Manual: Revised and Expanded. *Odessa, FL*: Psychological Assessment Resources.

Hecaen, H. (1972). Introduction to Neuropsychology. *Paris: Larousse*, 79(16), 5097-5100.

Heilman, K.M., Voeller, K., & Alexander, A.W. (1996). Developmental dyslexia: A Motor-articulatory Feedback Hypothesis. *Annals of Neurology*, 39, 407-412.

Henderson H.A., & Wachest, D. (2007). Temperament Theory and the Study of Cognition-emotion Interactions Across Development. *Developmental Review*, 27, 396-427.

Hermann, B.P., Wyler, A.R., & Richey, E.T. (1988). Wisconsin Card Sorting Test Performance in Patients with Complex Partial Seizures of Temporal-lobe Origin. *Journal of Clinical and Experimental Neurophysiology*, 10, 467-476.

Hermann, K. (1959). Reading Disability, a Medical Study of Word-blindness and Related Handicaps. *Springfield, IL*: Charles C. Thomas.

Hermann, K., & Norrie, E. (1958). Is Congenital word Blindness an Hereditary Type of Gerstmann's Syndrome? *Psychiatry and Neurology*, 136, 59-73.

Hinshelwood, J. (1907). Four Cases of Congenital Word Blindness Occurring in the Same Family. *British Medicd Joumai*, 2, 1229-1232.

Hinshelwood, J. (1909). Four Cases of Congenital Word-blindness Occurring in the Same Family. *British Medical Journal*, 2, 1229-1232.

Hinshelwood, J. (1911). Two Cases of Hereditary Word Blindness. *British Medical Joumd*, 1, 608-609.

Hinshelwood, J. (1917). *Congenital Word Blindness*. London: H.K. Lewis.

Hobson, P., & Leeds, L. (2001). Executive Functioning in Older People. *Reviews in Clinical Gerontology*, 11, 361-372.

Hooper, S.R., & Willis, W.G. (1989). *Learning Disabilities Subtyping: Neuro Psychological Foundations, Conceptual Models, and Issues in Clinical Differentiation*. New York: Springer - Verlag.

Horner, M.D., Flashman, L.A., Freides, D., Epstein, C.M., & Bakay, R.A. (1996). Temporal Lobe Epilepsy and Performance on the Wisconsin Card Sorting Test. *Journal of Clinical and Experimental Neuropsychology*, 18, 310-313.

Huizink, A. (2008). Prenatal Stress Exposure and Temperament: *A Review. European Journal of Developmental Science*, 2, 77-99.

Huston, A.M. (1992). *Understanding dyslexia: A Practical Approach for Parents and Teachers*. Lanham, MD: Madison Books.

Hutenlocher, P. (1991, September 26). Neural Plasticity. Paper Presented at the Brain Research Foundation Women's Council, University of Chicago.

Hynd, G.W., Conner, R.T., & Nieves, N. (1988). Learning Disabilities Subtypes: Perspectives and Methodological Issues in Clinical Assessment. New York: Plenum.

Igarashi, K., Oguni, H., Osawa, M., Awaya, Y., Kato, M., Mimura, M., *et al.* (2002). Wisconsin Card Sorting Test in Children with Temporal Lobe Epilepsy. *Brain & Development*, 24, 174-178.

Ilonen T., Leinonen K., Wallenius E., Karlsson H., Taiminen T., Salokangas R., Lauerma, H., *et al.*, (200). Impaired Wisconsin Card Sorting Test Performance in First-episode Severe Depression. *Nord J Psychiatry*; 54: 275-80.

Individuals with Disabilities Education Act of 1990, Public Law 101-476, 101st Congress.

Individuals with Disabilities Education Act of 1997, Public Law 105-17, 105th Congress, 1st sess. (January 7, 1997).

Individuals with Disabilities Education Improvement Act of 2004, Public Law 108-446, 108th Congress., 2nd sess. (December 3, 2004).

Jackson, E. (1906). Developmental alexia (Congenital Word Blindness). *American Journal of Medical Science.* 131, 843-849.

Joseph, J.E., Noble, K., & Eden, G.F. (2001). The Neurobiological basis of Reading. *Journal of Learning Disabilities*, 34, 566-579.

Jurado, B.M., & Rosselli, M. (2007). The Elusive Nature of Executive Functions: A Review of our Current Understanding. *Springer Science Business Media.* 17: 213-233.

Kapur, M. (1995). Mental Health of Indian Children. New Delhi: Sage Publication.

Kassubek, J., Juengling, F.D., Ecker, D., & Landwehrmeyer, G.B. (2005). Thalamic Atrophy in Huntington's Disease Co-varies with Cognitive Performance: A Morphometric MRI Analysis. *Cerebralcortex*, 15, 846-853.

Kauffman, J.M. (1994). Places of Change: Special Education's Power and Identify in an Era of Educational Reform. *Journal of Learning Disabilities*, 27, 610-618.

Kavale, K.A., & Forness, S.R. (2003). Learning Disability as a Discipline. In H.L. Swanson, K. R. Harris, & S. Graham (Eds.), *Handbook of Learning Disabilities*. New York, NY: Guilford.

Kawasaki, Y., Maeda, Y., Suzuki, M., Urata, K., Higashima, M., & Kiba, K., *et al*. (1993). e3SPECT Analysis of Regional Cerebral Blood Flow Changes in Patients with schizophrenia during the Wisconsin Card Sorting Test. *Schizophrenia Research*, 10, 109 116.

Keogh, B.K. (1983). Temparament: An Individual Difference of Importance in Intervention Programmes. *Topics in Early Childhood Special Education*, 2(2), 25-31.

Kephart, N.C. (1971). *The Slow Learner in the Classroom (2nd edn).* Columbus, O.H: Charles. E. Merrill.

Kerekes, N., Brändström, S., Lundstrom, S., Rastam, M., Nilsson, T., Anckarsater, H. (2013). ADHD, Autism Spectrum Disorder, Temperament, and Character: Phenotypical Associations and Etiology in a Swedish Childhood Twin Study, *Comprehensive Psychiatry*, 54(8), 1140-1147

Kerr, J. (1897). School Hygiene, in its Mental, Moral and Physical Aspects. Howard Medical Prize Essay, *Journd of the Royd Statistical Society*, 60, 613-680.

Kimberg, D.Y., D'Esposito, M., & Farah, M.J. (1997). Cognitive Functions in the Prefrontal Cortex-working Memory and Executive Control. *Current Directions in Psychological Science. American Psychological Society.* 6(6). 185-192. Retrieved from journals.sagepub.com

Kinsbourne, M., & Hiscock, M. (1981). Cerebral Lateralization and Cognitive Development: Conceptual & Methodological Issues. In G.W. Hynd J.E. Obrzut, *Neuropsychological Assessment and the School Age Child: Issues and Procedures* (pp. 125-166). New York: Grune & Stration.

Kinsbourne, M., & Warrington, E. (1966). Developmental Factors in Reading and Writing Backwardness. In Money, J. & Schiffman. G., *The Disabled Reader. Baltimore* : John Hopkins Press.

Kirk, S. (1963). *Educating Exceptional Children*. Boston: Houghton Miffin.

Knights, R.M., & Bakker D.J. (1976). *The Neuropsychology of Learning Disorder: Theoretical Approach*. Baltimore, MD: University Park Press.

Koechlin, E., Corrado, G., Pietrini, P., & Grafman, J. (2000). Dissociating the Role of the Medial and Lateral Anterior Prefrontal Cortex in Human Planning. *Proceedings of the National Academy of Science of the United States of America*, 97, 7651-7656.

Konishi, S., Hayashi, T., Uchida, I., Kikyo, H., Takahashi, E., & Miyashita, Y. (2002). Hemispheric Asymmetry in Human Lateral Prefrontal Cortex during Cognitive Set Shifting. *Proceedings of the National Academy of Sciences of the United States of America*, 99, 7803-7808.

Konishi, S., Jimura, K., Asari, T., & Miyashita, Y. (2003). Transient Activation of Superior Prefrontal Cortex during Inhibition of Cognitive Set. *The Journal of Neuroscience*, 23, 7776-7782.

Konishi, S., Nakajima, K., Uchida, I., Kameyama, M., Nakahara, K., & Sekihara, K., *et al*. (1998). Transient Activation of Inferior Prefrontal Cortex during Cognitive set Shifting. *Nature Neuroscience*, 1, 80-84.

Krathwohl, D.R. (1993). *Methods of Educational & Social Science Research: An Integrated Approach*. (1st Ed.). Waveland Press. New York: Longman, also Long Grove, IL.

Kraus, T.H. (2014). Pinpointing the Deficit in Executive Functions in Adolescents with Dyslexia Performing the Wisconsin Card Sorting Test: An ERP Study. *Journal of Learning Disabilities*. 47 (3). 208-223. Pennsylvania. Sage Publications. DOI: 10.1177|00222|94|2453084

Kretschmer, E. (1977). *Temperament und Character* (26edn.). Berlin: Springer
Kumar, J., & Suman, S. (2017). Identification and Prevalence of Learning Disabled Students. *International Journal of Scientific and Research Publications, Volume 7*, Issue 3, 317-319. Changing Minds. http:// changingminds.org/ explanations/personality/ personality_is.htm. (2008). (downloaded at 08 February 2008).

Kumari, V.M., & Barkiya, M.S. (2016). Children with Poor School Performance for Specific Learning Disability. *International Journal of Scientific Study, Vol 3*. Issue 12.

Kussmaul, A. (1877). Disturbance of Speech. *Cyclopedia of Practical Medicine, 14*, 581.

LaBuda, M.C., & DeFreis, J.C. (1990). Genetic Etiology of Reading Disability: Evidence from a Twin Study. In G. Th. Pavlidis (Ed.), *Perspectives on Dyslexia, Vol.1: Neurology, Neuropsychology and Genetics* (pp. 47-76). New York: John Wiley & Sons.

Larsen, R.J., & Buss, D.M. (2005). *Personality Psychology: Domains of Knowledge about Human Nature* (2nd ed.). Boston: McGraw-Hill.

Latzman, R.D. (2009). Interrelations among Youth Temperament, Executive Functions, and Externalizing Behaviors. Ph.D. (Doctor of Philosophy) Thesis, University of Iowa, 2009. http://ir.uiowa.edu/etd/306.

Leavell, C., & Lewandowski, L. (1990). Neurolinguistic Deficits and the Left Hemisphere in the Reading Disabled. *Developmental Neuropsychology*, 6(4), 319-337.

Lennerstrand, G., Ygge, J., & Jacobsson, C. (1993). Control of Binocular Eye Movements in Normals and Dyslexics. *Annals of the New York Academy of Sciences*, 682, 231-239.

Lerner, J. (2003). *Learning Disabilities: Theories, Diagnosis, and Teaching Strategies.* Boston: Houghton Mifflin.

Lerner, J.W. (1993). *Learning Disabilities: Theories Diagnosis and Teaching Strategies (6th ed.).* Boston: Houghton Mifflin.

Leskela, M., Hietanen, M., Kalska, H., Ylikoski, R., Pohjasvaara, T., & Mantyla, R., *et al.* (1999). Executive Functions and Speed of Mental Processing in Elderly Patients with Frontal or Nonfrontal Ischemic Stroke. *European Journal of Neurology*, 6, 653-661.

Levin. H.S. (1979). *The Acalculias, in Clinical Neuropsychology (eds. K.M. Heilan and E. Valenstein).* Oxford: Oxford University Press.

Lezak, M.D. (1983). *Neuropsychological Assessment (2nd Ed.).* New York: Oxford University Press.

Lezak, M.D., Howieson, D.B., & Loring, D.W. (2004). *Neuropsychological Assessment (4th Ed.*). New York: Oxford University Press.

Lezak, M.D., Howieson, D.M., & Loring, D.W. (2004). Neuropsychological Assessment (4th ed.). New York: Oxford University Press Lezak, M.D. (1995). *Neuropsychological Assessment* (3rd ed.). New York: Oxford University Press.

Lezak, M.D., Howieson, D.M., & Loring, D.W. (2004). *Neuropsychological Assessment (4th Ed.).* New York: Oxford University Press.

Lie, C. H., Specht, K., Marshall, J.C., & Fink, G.R. (2006). Using fMRI to Decompose the Neural Processes Underlying the Wisconsin Card Sorting Test. *Neuroimage*, 30, 1038-1049.

Light, J.G., DeFries, J.C., & Olson, R.K. (1998). Multivariate Behavioural Genetic Analysis of Achievement and Cognitive measures in Reading-disabled and Control Twin Pairs. *Human Biology,* 70, 215-237.

Livingstone, M. (1993). Parallel Processing in the Visual System and the Brain: Is One Subsystem Selectively affected in Dyslexia? In A.M. Galaburda (Ed.), *Dyslexia and Development: Neurobiological Aspects of Extra-ordinary Brains* (pp. 237-256). London: Harvard University Press.

Loehlin, J.C., & Nichols, J. (1976). Heredity, Environment and Personality. Austin: University of Texas.

Lombardi, W.J., Andreason, P.J., Sirocco, K.Y., Rio, D.E., Gross, R.E., & Umhau, J.C., *et al.* (1999). Wisconsin Card Sorting Test Performance Following Head Injury: Dorsolateral Fronto-striatal Circuit Activity Predicts Perseveration. *Journal of Clinical and Experimental Neuro Physiology,* 21, 2-16.

Lovegrove, W. (1993). Weakness in the Transient Visual System: A Causal Factor in Dyslexia? *Annals of the New York Academy of Sciences,* 682, 57-69.

Lubs, H.A., Rabin, M., Feldman, E., Jallad, B.J., Kushch, A., & Gross-Glenn, K. (1993). Familial dyslexia: Genetic and Medical Findings in Eleven Three-generation Families. *Annals of Dyslexia,* 43, 44-60.

Luria, A.R. (1973). *The Working Brain: An Introduction to Neuropsychology.* New York (NY): Basic Books.

Luria. R. (1966). *Higher Cortical Functions in Man.* New York: Basic Books.

Luzia Flavia Coelho, Maria Conceição do Rosário, Rosana Savio Mastrorosa, Monica Carolina Miranda, Orlando Francisco Amodeo Bueno. *(2012)* Performance of a Brazilian Sample on the Computerized Wisconsin Card Sorting Test *Psychology & Neuroscience, 2012, 5, 2, 147-156 DOI:10.3922/ j.psns.2012.2.04*

Lyon, G. R. (1996). Learning Disabilities. *The Future of Children,* 6(1), 54-76.

MacMillan, D.L. (1993). Development of Operational Definitions in Mental Retardation: Similarities and Differences with the Field of Learning Disabilities. In G.R. Lyon, D.B. Gray, J.F.

Macmillan., Gresham., Siperstein., & Bocian. Responsiveness to Intervention: An Alternative Approach to the Identification of Learning Disabilities. [Online].1996 [cited 2006 Apr]; [169].

Madeleine, W.M.C. (1986). Educating Children with Learning Problems: A Shared Responsibility. *Sage Journals,* 52(5), 411-415. Http://doi.org/ 10.1177/001 440298605200502.

Mardaga, S., & Hansenne, M. (2007). Relationships between Cloninger's Biosocial Model of Personality and the Behavioural Inhibition/Approach Systems (BIS/BAS). *Personality and Individual Differences,* 42, 715-722.

Marenco, S., Coppola, R., Daniel, D.G., Zigun, J.R., & Weinberger, D.R. (1993). Regional Cerebral Blood Flow during the Wisconsin Card Sorting Test in Normal Subjects Studied by xenon-133 Dynamic SPECT: Comparison of Absolute Values, Percent Distribution Values, and Covariance Analysis. *Psychiatry Research*, 50, 177-192.

Martel, M.M., Nigg, J.T., & Lucas, R.E. (2008). Trait Mechanisms in Youth with and without Attention-Deficit/Hyperactivity Disorder. Journal of Research in Personality, 42, 895-913.

Mather, N., & Roberts, R. (1994). Learning Disabilities: A Field In Danger of Extinction? *Learning Disabilities Research and Practice*, 9, 49-58.

McCrae, R.R., & John, O.P. (1992). An Introduction to the Five Factor Model and its Applications. Journal of Personality, 60, 175-215.

McKeever, W.F., & Van Deventer, A.D. (1975). Dyslexic Adolescents: Evidence of Impaired Visual and Auditory Language Processing. *Cortex*, 11, 361-378.

Mentzel, H.J., Gaser, C., Volz, H.P., Rzanny, R., Hager, F., & Sauer, H., *et al.* (1998). Cognitive Stimulation with the Wisconsin Card Sorting Test: Functional MR Imaging at 1.5 T. *Radiology*, 207, 399-404.

Mercer, C.D. (1991). *Students with Learning Disabilities (4th ed.).* New York: Macmillan.

Mercer, C.D., & Pullen, P.C. (2009). *Students with Learning Disabilities.* USA. Person Education Ltd.

Miller, E.K. (2000). The Prefrontal Cortex and Cognitive Control. *Nature Reviews Neuroscience*, 1 (1), 59-65.doi:10.1038/35036228

Milner, B. (1963). Effects of Different Brain Lesions on Card Sorting. *Archives of Neurology*, 9, 90-100.

Moats, L.C., & Lyon, G.R. (1993). Learning Disabilities in the United States: Advocacy, Science, and the Future of the Field. *Journal of Learning Disabilities*, 26, 282-294.

Mogasale, V.V., Patil, V.D., Patil, N.M. *et al.* (2012). Prevalence of Specific Learning Disabilities Among Primary School Children in a South Indian City. *Indian Journal of Pediatrics. Volume 79*, Issue 3, pp. 342-347.

Monchi, O., Petrides, M., Petre, V., Worsley, K., & Dagher, A. (2001). Wisconsin Card Sorting Revisited: Distinct Neural Circuits Participating in Different stages of the task identified by event-related functional magnetic resonance imaging. *The Journal of Neuroscience, 21*, 7733–7741.

Monchi, O., Petrides, M., Strafella, A. P., Worsley, K. J., & Doyon, J. (2006). Functional Role of the Basal Ganglia in the Planning and Execution of Actions. *Annuals of Neurology*, 59, 257-264.

Morais, D.B. (2000). Reconceptualization of Loyalty under a Resource Investment Perspective: Service Industry. Unpublished Doctroral Dissertation., Clemson University.

Morgan, W.P. (1896). A Case of Congenital word-blindness. *British Medical Journal, 11,* 378.

Moss, H.B., Blackston, T.C., Martin, C., & Tarter, R.E. (1992). Heightened Motor Activity in Male Offspring of Substance Abusing Fathers: Association with Temperament, Behaviour and Psychiatric Diagnosis. Biological Psychiatry, 32, 1135-1147.

Mukhopadhyay, P., Dutt, A., Kumar Das, S., Basu, A., Hazra, A., & Dhibar, T., *et al.* (2008). Identification of Neuroanatomical Substrates of Set-shifting Ability: Evidence from Patients with Focal brain Lesions. *Progress in Brain Research,* 168, 95-104.

Nagahama, Y., Fukuyama, H., Yamauchi, H., Katsumi, Y., & Magata, Y., Shibasaki, H., *et al.* (1997). Age-related Changes in Cerebral Blood Flow Activation during a Card Sorting Test. *Experimental Brain Research,* 114, 571-577.

Nagahama, Y., Fukuyama, H., Yamauchi, H., Matsuzaki, S., Konishi, J., & Shibasaki, H., *et al.* (1996). Cerebral Activation during Performance of a Card Sorting Test. *Brain,* 119, 1667-1675.

Nagahama, Y., Sadato, N., Yamauchi, H., Katsumi, Y., Hayashi, T., & Fukuyama, H., *et al.* (1998). Neural Activity during Attention Shifts between Object Features. *Neuroreport,* 9, 2633-2638.

National Joint Committee on Learning Disabilities. (1981). *Learning Disabilities: Issues on Definition*. Unpublished Manuscript. (Available from the Orton Dyslexia Society,724 York Road, Baltimore, MD 21204).

National Joint Committee on Learning Disabilities. (1988). [Letter to NJCLD Member Organisations.]

Nelson, H.E. (1976). A Modified Card Sorting Test Sensitive to Frontal Lobe Defects. *Cortex,* 12, 313-324.

Nettle, D. (2006). The Evolution of Personality Variation in Humans and other Animals. *Am. Psychol.* 61, 622-631. (Doi: 10. 1037/0003-066X.61. 6.622)

Njiokiktjien, C. (1994). Dyslexia: A Neuro Scientific Puzzle. Acta *Paedopsychiatrica,* 56, 157-167.

Norman, D.A., & Shallice, T. (1986). Attention to Action: Willed and Automatic Control of Behaviour. In R.J. Davidson, *et al.* (Ed.) *Consciousness and Self-regulation* (Vol. 4, (pp. 1-18)). New York: Plenum.

Norris, G., & Tate, R. (2000). The Behavioral Assessment of the Dysexecutive Syndrome (BADS): Ecological, Concurrent and Construct Validity. *Neuro Psychological Rehabilitation,* 11, 33-45.

Ogden, J.A. (1996). Phonological dyslexia and Phonological Dysgraphia following Left and Right Hemispherectomy. *Neuropsychologia*, 34(9), 905-918.

Ojemann, C.A. (1974). Mental Arithmetic during Human Thalamic Stimulation. *Neuropsychologia*, 12, 1-10.

Olson. R.K., Wise. B., Conners. F., Rack, J. & Fulker, D. (1989). *Specific Deficits in Component Reading and Language Skills: Genetic and Environmental Influences*. Journal of Learning Disabilities, 22, 339-348.

Orton, S.T. (1928). Specific Reading Disability - strephosymbolia. *Journal of the American Medical Association*, 90, 1095-1009.

Orton, S.T. (1937). *Reading, Writing, and Speech Problems in Children*. New York: W.W. Norton.

Parellada, E., Catafau, A.M., Bernardo, M., Lomena, F., Catarineu, S., & Gonzalez-Monclus, E. (1998). The Resting and Activation Issue of Hypofrontality: A Single Photon Emission Computed Tomography Study in Neuroleptic-naive and Neuroleptic-free Schizophrenic Female Patients. *Biological Psychiatry*, 44, 787-790.

Parkin, A., & Java, R. (1999). Deterioration of Frontal Lobe Function in Normal Aging: Influences of Fluid Intelligence versus Perceptual Speed. *Neuro psychology*, 13, 539-545.

Parucka, M.A. (1972). An Investigation of Concept Formation in Children with Learning Disabilities. *Texas Tech University*.

Pauls. D.L. (1996). Genetic Linkage Studies. In G.R. Lyon (Chair), *Critical Discoveries in Learning Disabilities: A Summary of Findings by NIH Research Programs in Learning Disabilities*. Workshop Conducted at the Learning Disability Association International Conference, Dallas.

Pennington, B.F. (1991). *Diagnosing Learning Disorders: A Neuropsychological Framework*. New York: Guilford Press.

Pennington, B.F. (1995). Genetics of Learning Disabilities. *Journal of Child Neurology, 10* (Suppl. 1), S69-77.

Pennington, B., Smith, S., Kimberling, W., Greene, P., & Haith, M. (1987). Left-handedness and Immune Disorders in Familial Dyslexics. *Archives of Neurology*, 44, 634-639.

Pennington. B.F., Bender. B., Puck. M., Salbenblatt, J. & Robinson. A. (1982). Learning Disabilities in Children with Sex Chromosome Anomalies. *Child Development*, 53, 1182-1192.

Perrine, K. (in Press,). Differential Aspects of Conceptual Processing in the Category Test and Wisconsin Card Sorting Test. *Journal of Clinical and Experimental Neuropsychology*.

Petrill, S.A., Deckard, K.D., Thompson, L.A., DeThrone, L.S., & Schatschneider. (2006). Reading Skills in Early Readers: Genetic and Shared Environmental Influences. *Journal of Learning Disabilities*, 39(1), 48-55.

Petrill, S., Kovas, Y., Hart, S.A., Thompson, L.A., & Plomin, R. (in press). The Genetic and Environmental Etiology of High Math Performance in 10-year-old. *Developmental Science.*

Pirzzolo, F.J., & Rayner, K. (1979). Cerebral Organization and Reading Diability. Neuropsychologia, 17, 485-491.

Poeppel, D. (1996). A Critical Review of PET Studies of Phonological Processing. *Brain and Language,* 55, 317-351.

Posner, M.I., & Raichle, M.E. (1996). *Images of Mind.* New York, NY: Scientific American Library.

Poustka, L., Bender, F., Bock, M., Bolte, S., Mohler, E., Banaschewski, T., & Goth, K. (2011). Personality and Social Responsiveness in Autism Spectrum Disaorders and Attention Deficit/Hyperactivity Disorder. *Zeitschrifit Fur Kinder-Und Jugedpsychiatrie and Psychotherapie,* 39, 133-141(In German)

Pronsnick, K.P., Evans, W.J., & Farris, J.R. (2003). Development and Psychometric Properties of Score from the Short Index of Self-directedness. *Measurement and Evaluation in Counselling and Development,* 36, 76-82. Retrieved from http:// www.innopac.up.ac.za

Pugh, K.R., Shaywitz, B.A., Shaywitz, S.E., Constable, T.R., Skudlarski, P., & Fullbright, R. K., *et al.* (1996). Cerebral Organization of Component Processes in Reading. *Brain,* 119, 1221-1238.

Purper-Ouakil, D., Cortese, S., Wohl, M., Aubron, V., Orejarena, S., Michel, G., & Gorwood, P. (2010). Temperament and Character Dimensions Associated with Clinical Characteristics and Treatment Outcome in Attention-deficit/Hyperactivity Disorder Boys. *Comprehensive psychiatry,* 51, 286-292.

Purper-Ouakil, Diane & Ramoz., Nicolas & Lepagnol-Bestel., Aude-Marie & Gorwood., Philip & Simonneau, Michel (2010). Neurobiology of Attention Deficit/Hyperactivity Disorder. *Pediatric Research.* 69. 69R-76R. 10.1203/PDR.0b013e318212b40f.https://www.researchgate.net

Ragland, J.D., Gur, R.C., Glahn, D.C., Censits, D.M., Smith, R.J., & Lazarev, M.G., *et al.* (1998). Frontotemporal Cerebral Blood Flow Change during Executive and Declarative Memory Tasks in Schizophrenia: A Positron Emission Tomography Study. *Neuropsychology,* 12, 399-413.

Raskind, W.H. (2001). Current Understanding of the Genetic basis of Reading and Spelling Disability. *Learning Disability Quarterly,* 24, 141-157.

Read, C. (1981). Writing is not the Inverse of Reading in Young Children. In Federicksen, C., & Dominic, J.F., *Writing: The Nature Development & Teaching of Written Communication.*

Richardson, E., DiBenedeton, B., & Bradley, C.M. (1977). The Relationship of Sound Blending to Reading Achievement. *Review of Educational Research,* 47, 319-334.

Roberts, A.C., Robins, T.W., & Weiskrantz, L. (1996). Executive and Cognitive Functions of the Prefrontal Cortex. *Phil Trans Royal Soc Lond Series B*, 351, 1387-1527.

Robinson, A.L., Heaton, R.K., Lehman, R.A., & Stilson, D.W. (1980). The Utility of the Wisconsin Card Sorting Test in Detecting and Localizing Frontal Lobe Lesions. *Journal of Consulting and Clinical Psychology*, 48, 605-614.

Rochette, É., & Bernier, A. (2016). Parenting and Preschoolers' Executive Functioning: A Case of Differential Susceptibility? *International Journal of Behavioural Development*, 40, 151-161.

Rogers, R.D., Andrews, T.C., Grasby, P.M., Brooks, D.J., & Robbins, T.W. (2000). Contrasting Cortical and Subcortical Activations Produced by Attentional-set Shifting and Reversal Learning in Humans. *Journal of Cognitive Neuroscience*, 12, 142-162.

Rogoff, B. (1990). Apprenticeship in thinking Cognitive Development in Social Context. New York: Oxford University Press.

Rothbart K.M. (2011). Becoming Who We Are: Temperament and Personality in Development. Guilford Publications. https://www.guilford.com/excerpts/rothbart.pdf.

Rothbart M.K., & Bates, J.E. (1998). Temperament. In W. Damon (Series Editor) and N. Eisenberg (Volume Editor), Social, Emotional, and Personality Development: Vol. 3, Handbook of Child Psychology (pp. 105-176). New York: Willey.

Rothbart, M.K. (2007). Temperament, Development, and Personality. *Association for Psychological Science, 16 (4)*, 207-212.

Rothbart, M.K., & Bates, J.E. (1998).Temperament. In W. Damon (Series Ed.) & N. Eisenberg (Vol. Ed.), *Handbook of Child Psychology:* Vol. 3, *Social, Emotional, and Personality Development* (5th ed., pp. 105-176). New York: Wiley.

Rothbart, M.K., & Bates, J.E. (2006). Temperament (6th Ed. In N. Eisenberg, W., Damon & R. Lerner (Eds.)). *Handbook of Child Psychology: Social, Emotional and Personality Development*, 3, 99-116. Hoboken, NJ: Willey.

Rothbart, M.K., & Bates, J.E. (2006). Temperament. In W. Damon & R. Lerner (Series Eds.), & N. Eisenberg (Vol. Ed.), Handbook of Child Psychology, Vol. 3. Social, Emotional, and Personality Development (6th ed., pp. 99-166). New York: Wiley.

Rothbart, M.K., & Derryberry, D. (1981). Development of Individual Difference in Temperament. In M. Lamb & A. Brown (Eds.), Advances in Developmental Psychology. Boston: Erlbaum.

Rothbart, M.K., Ahadi, S.A., & Hershey, K.L. (1994). Temperament and Social Behaviour in Childhood. *Merrill-Palmer Quarterly*, 40, 21-39.

Rothbart, M.K., Ahadi, S.A., Hershey, K.L., & Fisher, P. (2001). Investigations of Temperament at Three to Seven Years: The Children's Behaviour Questionnaire. *Child Development*, 72(5), 1394-1408.

Rothbart, M.K., Ellis, L.K., & Posner, M.J. (2004). Temperament and Self-regulation. In R.F. Baumeister & K.D. Vohs (Eds.), *Handbook of Self-regulation: Research, Theory and Applications.* (pp. 357-370). New York: Guilford Press.

Rourke, B.P. (1985). *Neuropsychology of Learning Disabilities: Essentials of Subtype Analysis.* New York: Guilford Press.

Rourke, B.P. (1995). *Syndrome of Nonverbal Learning Disabilities: Neuro Developmental: Neurodevelopmental Manifestations.* New York: Guilford Press.

Rourke. B.P. (1985). *Neuropsychology of Learning Disabilities: Essentials of Subtype Analysis.* New York: Guilford Press.

Rourke. B.P., & Conway, J.A. (1997). Disabilities of Arithmetic and Mathematical Reasoning: Perspectives from Neurology and Neuro Psychology. *Journal of Learning Disabilities*, 30(1), 34-46.

Rourke. B.P., & Fuerst, D.R. (1992). Psychosocial Dimensions of Learning Disability Subtypes: Neuropsychological Studies in the Windsor Laboratory. *School Psychology Review*, 21, 361-374.

Rourke. B.P., & Fuerst, D.R. (1995). Cognitive Processing, Academic Achievement, and Psychosocial Functioning: A Neurodevelopmental Perspective. In D. Cicchetti & D.J. Cohen (Eds.), *Developmental Psychopathology* Vol. 1: Theory and methods (pp. 391-423). New York: John Wiley & Sons.

Rourke. B.P., & Fuerst, D.R. (1996). Psychosocial Dimensions of Learning Disability Subtypes. *Assessment*, 3(3), 277-290.

Royall, P., Lauterbach, E.C., Cummings, J.L., Reeve, A., Rummans, T.A., & Kaufer, D.I., *et al.* (2002). Executive Control Function: A Review of its Promise and Challenges for Clinical Research. *Journal of Neuropsychiatry and Clinical Neuroscience*, 14, 377-405.

Russo, M.F., Stokes, G.S., Lashy, B.B., Christ, M. AG., McBurnett, K., Loeber, R., Green, S. M. (1993). A Sensation Seeking Scale for Children: Further Refinement and Psychometric Development. *Journal of Psychopathology and Behavioural Assessment*,15, 69-86.

Salthouse, T.A. (2005). Relations between Cognitive Abilities and Measures of Executive Functioning. *Neuropsychology*, 19(4), 532-545. doi:10.1037/0894-4105.19.4.532

Satz, P. (1990). Developmental Dyslexia: An Etiological Reformulation. In G.T. Pavlidis (Ed.), Perspectives on Dyslexia (Vol. 1, pp. 3-26). New York, John Wiley and Sons, Inc.

Satz, P., Taylor, H.G., Friel, J., & Fletcher, J.M. (1978). Some Developmental and Predictive Precursors of Reading Disability: Six Year Follow- up. In A.L. Benton & D. Pearl, Dyslexia: *An Appraisal of Current Knowledge.* New York: Oxford University Press.

Saucier, G., & Goldberg, L.R. (1996a). The Language of Personality: Lexical Perspectives on the Five-factor Model. In J.S. Wiggins (Ed.), The Five-factor Model of Personality: Theoretical Perspectives. (pp. 21-50): Guilford Press, New York, NY, US.

Shalev, R.S., Manor, O., Amir, N., Wertman-Elad, R., & Gross-Tsur, V. (1995). Developmental dyscalculia and Brain Laterality. *Cortex*, 31, 357-365.

Shaywitz, S.E. (1998). Current Concepts: Dyslexia. *New England Journal of Medicine*, 338(5), 307-312.

Sigvardsson, S., Cloninger, C.R., Bohman, M., & Von Knorring, A.L. (1982). Predisposition to Petty Criminality in Swedish Adoptees. III. Sex Differences and Validation of the Male Typology. *Archives of General Psychiatry*, 39, 1248-1253.

Sigvardsson, S., Von Knorring, A.L., Bohman, M., Cloninger, C.R. (1984). An Adoption Study of Somatoform Disorders. I. The Relationship of Somatization to Psychiatric Disability. *Archives of General Psychiatry*, 41, 853-859.

Sinatra, G.M., Brem, S.K., & Evans, E.M. (2008). Changing Minds? Implications of Conceptual Change for Teaching and Learning about Biological Evolution. Evolution: Education and Outreach, 1, 189-195.

http://dx.doi.org/10.1007/s12052-008-0037-8

Slaghuis, W.L., Lovegrove, W.J., & Davidson, J.A. (1993). Visual and Language Processing Deficits are Concurrent in Dyslexia. *Cortex*, *29*, 601-615.

Slaghuis, W.L., Lovegrove, W.J., & Davidson, J.A. (1993). Visual and Language Processing Deficits are Concurrent in Dyslexia. *Cortex*, *29*, 601-615.

Slaghuis, W.L., Twell, A.J., & Kingston, K.R. (1996). Visual and Language Processing Disorders are Concurrent in dyslexia and Continue into Adulthood. *Cortex*, 32, 413-438.

Smith, C.R. (1994). *Learning Disabilities: The Interaction of Learner; Task, and Setting* (3rd ed.). Boston: Allyn & Bacon.

Smith, E.E., & Jonides, J. (1999). Storage and Executive Processes in the Frontal Lobes. *Science*, 283,1657-1661.doi:10.1126/SCIENCE.283. 5408. 1657.

Smith, S.D., Kimberling, W.J., & Pennington, B.F. (1991). Screening for Multiple Genes Influencing dyslexia. Reading and Writing: *An Inter Disciplinary Journal*, 3, 285-298.

Smith. S.D., Kimberling. W.J., & Pennington, B.F. (1991). Screening for Multiple Genes Influencing Dyslexia. *Reading & Writing*, 3(3-4), 285-298.

Stein, J.F. (1996). Visual System and Reading. In C.H. Chase, G.D. Rosen, & G.F. Sherman (Eds.), *Developmental dyslexia: Neural, Cognitive, and Genetic Mechanisms* (pp. 107-125). Baltimore, MD: York Press.

Stephenson, S. (1907). Six Cases of Congenital Word-blindness Affecting Three Generations of One Family. *Ophthalmoscope*, 5, 482-484.

Stephenson. (1905). Six Cases of Congenital Word - Blindness Affecting Three Generation of our Family. *Ophthalmoscope*, 5, 482-484.

Strauss, E., Hunter, M., & Wada, J. (1993). Wisconsin Card Sorting Performance: Effects of Age of Onset of Damage and Laterality of Dysfunction. *Journal of Clinical and Experimental Neurophysiology*, 15, 896-902.

Strauss, E., Sherman, E.M.S., & Spreen, O. (2006). *A Compendium of Neuropsychological Tests: Administration, Norms, and Commentary (3rd Ed.).* New York: Oxford University Press.

Strelau, J. (1998). *Temperament: A Psychological Perspective*. Hingham, MA, USA: Kluwer Academic Publishers.

Stromswold, K. (2001). The Heritability of Language: A Review and Metaanalysis of Twin, Adoption and Linkage Studies. *Language*, 77, 647–723.

Studdert-Kennedy, M., & Mody, M. (1995). Auditory Temporal Perception Deficits in the Reading-impaired: A Critical Review of the Evidence. *Psychonomic Bulletin & Review*, 2, 508-514.

Stuss, D. (1992). Biological and Physiological Development of Executive Function. Brain and Cognition, 20, 8-23.

Stuss, D.T., & Alexander, M. (2000). Executive Functions and the Frontal Lobes: A Conceptual View. *Psychological Research*, 63, 289-298.

Stuss, D.T., & Benson, D.F. (1986). *The Frontal Lobes*. New York: Raven.

Stuss, D.T., Levine, B., Alexander, M.P., Hong, J., Palumbo, C., & Hamer, L., *et al.* (2000). *Wisconsin Card Sorting Test Performance in Patients with Focal Frontal and Posterior Brain Damage: Effects of Lesion Location and Test Structure on Separable Cognitive Processes. Neuropsychologia*, 38, 388-402.

Stuss, D.T., Levine, B., Alexander, M.P., Hong, J., Palumbo, C., & Hamer, L., *et al.* (2002). Wisconsin Card Sorting Test performance in Patients with Focal Frontal and Posterior Brain Damage: Effects of Lesion Location and Test Structure on Separable Cognitive Processes. *Neuropsychologia*, 38, 388-402.

Suchy, Y. (2009). Executive Functioning: Overview, Assessment, and Research Issues for Non-neuropsychologists. *Annals of Behavioural Medicine*, 37, 106-116.doi:10.1007/s12160-009-9097-4

Svrakic, D.M., Draganic, S., Hill, K., Bayon, C., Przybeck, T.R., & Cloninger, C.R. (2002), Temperament, Character, and Personality Disorders: Etiologic, Diagnostic, Treatment Issues. *Acta Psychiatrica Scandinavica*, 106: 189-195. doi: 10.1034/j.1600-0447.2002.02196.x

Tallal, P., Miller, S., & Fitch, R.H. (1993). Neurobiological basis of Speech: A Case for the Pre-eminence of Temporal Processing. *Annals of the New York Academy of Sciences*, 682, 27-47.

Tarter, R.E. (1988). Are there Inherited Behavioural Traits that Predispose to Substance Abuse? *Journal of Consulting & Clinical Psychology*, 56(2), 189-196.

Teglasi, H, Cohn, A., & Meshbesher, N. (2004). Temperament and Learning Disability. *Winter*, Volume 27, 12-13.

Telzrow, C.R., & Bonar, A.M. (2002). Responding to Students with Nonverbal Learning Disabilities. *Teaching Exceptional Children*, 34, 8-13.

Teuber, H.L., Battersby, W.S., & Bender, M.B. (1951). Performance of Complex Visual Tasks after Cerebral Lesions. The Journal of Nervous and Mental Disease, 114, 413-429. Thomas, G.J. (1905). Gongenital "Word-blindness" and its Treatment. *Ophthalmoscope* 3, 380-385.

The International Classification of Mental and Behavioural Disorders: *Clinical Descriptions and Diagnostic Guidelines*. (2004). World Health Organisation, Geneva, A.I.T.B.S. Publishers & Distributors, Delhi-51.

Thompson, L.A., Detterman, D.K., & Plomin, R. (1991). Associations between Cognitive Abilities and Scholastic Achievement: Genetic Overlap but Environmental Differences. *Psychological Science*, 2, 158-165.

Tien, A.Y., Schlaepfer, T.E., Orr, W., & Pearlson, G.D. (1998). SPECT Brain Blood Flow Changes with Continuous Ligand Infusion during Previously Learned WCST Performance. *Psychiatry Research*, 82, 47-52.

Tranel, D., Hall, L.E., Olson, S., & Tranel, N.N. (1987). Evidence for a Right Hemisphere Developmental Learning Disability. *Developmental Neuro Psychology*, 3(2), 113-127.

Trites, R.L., & Fiedorowicz, C. (1976). Follow-up Study of Children with Specific (or Primary) Reading Disability. In *The Neuropsychology of Learning Disorders, Theoretical Approaches, ed.* R.M. Knights & D.J. Bakkar. Baltimore: University Park Press.

Tsuchiya E., Oli J., Yahara N., & Fujieda K. (2005). Computerized version of the Wisconsin Card Sorting Test in Children with High Functioning Autistic Disorder or Attention-deficit/Hyperactive Disorder. *Brain Dev*; 27: 233-6.

U.S. Office of Education. (1968). *First Annual Report of National Advisory Committee on Handicapped Children*. Washington, DC: U.S. Department of Health, Education, and Welfare.

U.S. Office of Education. (1977). Assistance to States for Education of Handicapped Children: Procedures for Evaluating Specific Learning Disabilities, 42 *fed.reg.65,082-65,085.*

Van den Broek, M.D., Bradshaw, C.M., & Szabadi, E. (1993). Utility of the Modified Wisconsin Card Sorting Test in Neuropsychological Assessment. The British Journal of *Clinical Psychology*, 32, 333-343.

Vellutino, F.R., Steger, J.A., Desetto, L., & Phillips, F. (1975). Immediate and Delayed Recognition of Visual Stimuli in Poor and Normal Readers. *Journal of Experimental Child Psychology*, 19, 223-232.

Vellutino, F.R. (1979). Dyslexia: Theory and Research. *Cambridge, MD*: MIT Press.

Voeller, K.K.S. (1995). Clinical Neurologic Aspects of the Right Hemisphere Deficit Syndrome. *Journal of Child Neurology, 10 (Suppl. 1)*, S16-22.

Volz, H.P., Gaser, C., Hager, F., Rzanny, R., Mentzel, H.J., & Kreitschmann-Andermahr, I., *et al.* (1997). Brain Activation during Cognitive Stimulation with the Wisconsin Card Sorting Test – A Functional MRI Study on Healthy Volunteers and Schizophrenics. *Psychiatry Research*, 75, 145-157.

Vygotsky, L. (1962). *Thought and Language*. Cambridge, MA: MIT Press.

Wachs, T.D. (2000). Linking Nutrition and Temperament and Personality Development Across the Life span edited by Molfeese, V.J., & Molfeese, D.L. Lawrence Erlbaum Associates, Publishers, New Jersy.

Wager, T.D., & Smith, E.E. (2003). Neuroimaging Studies of Working Memory: A Meta-analysis. *Behavioural Neuroscience*, 3, 241-253.

Wang, L., Kakigi, R., & Hoshiyama, M. (2001). Neural Activities during Wisconsin Card Sorting Test – MEG Observation. *Brain Research: Cognitive Brain Research*, 12, 19-31.

Welsh, M.C., & Pennington, B.F. (1988). Assessing Frontal Lobe Functioning in Children: Views from Developmental Psychology, 4, 199-230.

Welsh, M., Parke, R.D., Widaman, K., & O'Neil, R. (2001). Linkages between Children's Social and Academic Competence: A Longitudinal Analysis. Journal of School Psychology, 39, 463-482.

Williams, P.G., Suchy, Y., & Rau, H.K. (2009). Individual Differences in Executive Functioning: Implications for Stress Regulation. *Annals of Behavioural Medicine*, 3, 126-140.doi:1007/s12160-009-9100-02

Witelson, S. (1977). Developmental dyslexia: Two Right Hemispheres and None Left. *Science*, 195, 309-311.

Yee-Pay Wuanga., Chwen-Yng Su a., & Jui-Hsing Su. (2011). Wisconsin Card Sorting Test Performance in Children with Developmental Coordination Disorder. *Research in Developmental Disabilities* 32, 1669-1676.

Yoo, H.J., Kim, M., Ha, J.H., Chung, A., Sim, M.E., Kim, S.J., & Lyoo, I.K. (2006). Biogenetic Temperament and Character and Attention Deficit Hyperactivity Disorder in Korean Children. *Psychopathology*, 39, 25-31.

Zelazo, P.D., & Muller, U. (2002). Executive Function in Typical and Atypical Development. In U. Goswami (Ed.) *Blackwell Handbook of Childhood Cognitive Development* (pp. 445-469). Malden, MA: Blackwell.

Zelazo, P.D., Carter, A., Reznick, J., & Frye, D. (1997). Early Development of Executive Functions: A Problem-solving Framework. *Review of General Psychology*, 1, 198-226.

Zelazor, P.D., & Frye, D. (1998). II. Cognitive Complexity and Control: The Development of Executive Functions. *Current Direction in Psychological Science*, 7, 121-126.

Zentner, M., & Bates, J.E. (2008). *Child Temperament*. European Journal of Developmental Science, 2, 2-37.

Zerbin-Rudin, E. (1967). Congenital Word-blindness. *Bulletin of the Orton Society*, 17, 47-55.

Zuckerman, M. (1992). What is a basic Factor and which Factors are basic? Turtles all the way down. *Personality and Individual Differences*, 13(6), 675-681. doi:10.1016/0191-8869(92)90238-K.

Zuckerman, M. (1994) *Behavioural Expressions and Biosocial bases of Sensation Seeking*. New York: Cambridge University Press, 62.

Zuckerman, M., Kuhlman, D.M., Joireman, J., Teta, P., & Kraft, M. (1993). A Comparison of Three Structural Models for Personality: The Big Three, the Big Five, and the Alternative Five. *Journal of Personality and Social Psychology*, 65(4), 757-768. Retrieved from http://www.innopac.up.ac.za

https://kateswaffer.files.wordpress.com/2016/09/screen-shot-2016-0919-at-7-01-02-am.png

https://www.education.com/reference/article/temperament-emotional-behavioral-disorders

Landmark College, 2012 http://www.landmark.edu/ld-and-adhd-resources/learning-disabilities-and-differences/ProQuest Dissertations and National Center for Learning Disabilities, (2010) http://www.ld.org

Office of the Faculty Resources for Disabilities Portals and Pathways to Inclusive Instruction, 2002 (NJCLD, 1990)

http://www.ldonline.org/about/partners/njcld/archives

Reading Rockets, 2011 http://www.readingrockets.org/article/280/

Student Disability Services, 2001. John Hopkins University http://web.jhu.edu/disabilities/faculty/types_of_disabilities/learning.html

Theses, 2009. http://udini.proquest.com/view/tolerance-our-voice-an-elementary-pqid:1946931441/

www.dsf.net.ac

www.ldamerica.org

Index